MY HORIZONTAL LIFE

OTHER BOOKS BY AND ABOUT CHELSEA HANDLER

Lies That Chelsea Handler Told Me

Chelsea Chelsea Bang Bang

MY HORIZONTAL LIFE
A COLLECTION OF
ONE-NIGHT STANDS

CHELSEA HANDLER

A CHELSEA HANDLER BOOK /
BORDERLINE AMAZING® PUBLISHING

GRAND CENTRAL
PUBLISHING

NEW YORK   BOSTON

A Chelsea Handler Book/Borderline Amazing® Publishing

Grand Central Publishing
Hachette Book Group
1290 Avenue of the Americas
New York, NY 10104

www.HachetteBookGroup.com

Printed in the United States of America

10 9 8 7 6 5 4 3 2

RRD-C

Previously published in the United States by Bloomsbury in 2005.

First Trade Paperback Edition: July 2013

A Chelsea Handler Book/Borderline Amazing® Publishing is an imprint of Grand Central Publishing.
Grand Central Publishing is a division of Hachette Book Group, Inc.
The Grand Central Publishing name and logo is a trademark of Hachette Book Group, Inc.

The Hachette Speakers Bureau provides a wide range of authors for speaking events. To find out more, go to www.hachettespeakersbureau.com or call (866) 376-6591.

The publisher is not responsible for websites (or their content) that are not owned by the publisher.

ISBN 978-1-4555-7751-4

To my parents—
Thank you for having me.
Now look what I've done.

CONTENTS

MY HORIZONTAL LIFE

LOOK WHO'S HAVING SEX WITH MOMMY

I WAS SEVEN years old when my sister told me she'd give me five dollars to run upstairs into my parents' room while they were having sex and take a picture. At that age I had heard of sex but had no idea what it looked like. I knew for sure that my parents were sexually active. My father had impregnated my mother on six different occasions, all of which she decided to keep, so it was clear to my siblings and me that there was a definite attraction. There were many times when we would hear loud bumping and raucous laughter coming from their bedroom. My brothers and sisters always reacted with disgust and, being the youngest, I would follow suit, but was never sure why. Without knowing exactly what the act of sex entailed, there wasn't any real reason to be revolted, but it had become second nature to pretend I knew something I didn't.

I was always up for a chance to make easy money. I had been wearing hand-me-downs since I was born, and by the age of seven was already sick and tired of my second-string wardrobe. I may not have known what sex was, but I did know that I needed to step up my wardrobe in order to be taken seriously in the first grade. "No problem," I said. "Where's the camera and how do I use it?"

I tiptoed up the stairs leading to my parents' bedroom with my sister Sloane following close behind. Their door had a lock on it, but it was old and didn't secure inside the doorjamb anymore. If it was locked you weren't able to turn the handle, but if you smashed your body into it, it would open.

I checked and saw it was locked. I would have to use physical force. Sloane crept back toward the top of the staircase. I set up for a running start.

"Ready?" I asked her.

"Go!" she whispered.

Seeing your mother naked is not something you easily recover from. Seeing your mother naked and jumping from one side of a king-size bed to the other with a nurse's hat on while your father, who is also naked, is chasing her with a bandanna around his neck is reason to put yourself up for adoption. Fortunately, I took the first picture before anything had a chance to register. The second picture was of my father heading toward me with a belt.

My sister was already down the stairs when I came running out of my parents' room. I jumped all the way from the top of the stairs to the bottom. Luckily, I had perfected this jump months earlier during three consecutive snow days. I did not dare look behind me to see if my father and his penis were chasing me; I just kept running. We lived in a split-level house, so at the bottom of the big stairs, there was a shorter set of stairs to the right and to the left. I went left and my sister went right. I saw her head for the basement and followed her in. Our basement doubled as the laundry room; the one room in our house my father had never been in.

"Lock the door!" she barked, as she scrambled to hide under a pile of dirty clothes.

"Oh, my God, Dad has a belt," I told her.

"What?"

"A belt! He has a belt! I think he wants to hit us with it!"

"The one he wears with his pants?" she asked.

"Yes," I said. "I think he wants to belt us!"

We were too scared to cry. This was it for me, I was sure of it. I was going to be murdered in my basement by my naked father, with a belt. I had never been hit by a belt before but had heard stories about it happening in poorer neighborhoods. Suddenly, there was the sound of footsteps coming down the stairs and then banging on the door.

"Open the goddamn door! Now! You two are gonna get a smack and you're gonna get it now!"

I stared at Sloane with big eyes. I wanted her to think of a way out of this mess. She was twelve and she needed to take charge.

"Ask him if it's with the belt or his hand," Sloane said.

I looked at her to make sure she was serious, then yelled back, "With your hand or a belt?"

"What?!"

I went closer to the stairs that led to the door. "Are you going to hit us with the belt or your hand?"

He was shaking the handle now. "No one's getting hit with a belt!" he shouted. "One...two..."

This was before there were time-outs, so my sister and

I didn't know what to make of his counting. I wondered if his ABCs were next. He stopped at "three," and we braced ourselves when "four" didn't come.

Sloane was holding on to me for dear life. Her crying had turned into heaving, and now she started to shake uncontrollably. I tried to comfort her by rubbing her back like my mother did but was too preoccupied with my imminent beating to be very reassuring.

Since my sister had turned into a real mess, it was up to me to devise a plan of escape. At that moment, Sloane wouldn't have been able to lead a horse to our swimming pool, never mind leading me to my bedroom without getting my ass kicked.

"We have to go up and just let him hit us," my sister whispered.

"Ah, I don't think so. I don't make appointments to get hit. Plus, this was your idea and Dad should hit you both times."

"I want to get it over with!"

"No fucking way. I am not going upstairs to get hit."

This was the very first time I said "fucking" in front of anyone and I liked the way it sounded. I had heard my brothers and sisters use curse words but had never dared use one myself in front of anyone. But I had practiced alone in my room lots of times, trying out different cadences and intonations: "Fuck, fuck, fuck you, fucknut. Shit, shitstain, fucker! Go fuck a duck, you asswipe!" My favorite was, "What a fucking cocksucker." The plan was to say this casually to one of my new friends while one of our teachers walked by. No one in kindergarten ever really got my sense of humor, so I was hell-bent on making my mark in the first grade.

Saying the word "fucking" in front of my sister catapulted me to an instant state of authority. Sloane stared expectantly at me. I strained to hear what was going on upstairs. Suddenly, everything was very quiet. I fantasized that my father had forgotten why he had wanted to hit us in the first place. Maybe he was watching the stock market and found out that his eight shares of Noah's Bagels had quadrupled. Maybe if we stayed down there long enough he would forget all about what we did and actually be excited to see us when we came out. I could lie and say I was just looking for Q-tips and used the camera to block what I hadn't expected to see. Or I could say I just wanted help with my homework. My father loved when I did my homework.

We hadn't even been in the basement for a whole half hour when my sister started to complain that she was hungry.

"Where do you think Mom is?" she asked. My mother was the nice one, and she always protected us when my father was in one of his moods. I knew my mother wouldn't be mad at us because she was always defending us to our father no matter what we did. Especially since we had a lot to hold over her head.

All I would have to do is remind her of a week earlier when she forgot to pick me up from school and I had been accosted by a male predator on my way home. Our house wasn't even a mile from school, but some man slowed his car along the sidewalk I was walking on and asked if I knew any tricks. Upon taking a good look at an overweight older man with gray stubble, wearing a pair of coveralls, I bolted home faster than I'd finished the fifty-yard dash earlier that day. After a good twenty minutes of me berating my mother for not picking me up and allowing me to possibly be abducted, she hit the roof.

"But you weren't, were you?" she said. "Luckily you were able to outrun him!"

My mother is European and expresses her love through food and cuddling. She wasn't the type of mother who would make it to school plays or soccer games, but if you wanted to stay home sick, she was your girl. Whenever you'd go up to her room to cuddle with her, she'd pull out a KitKat or Snickers bar from her night table and look at you with dancing eyes. She is a very sweet woman but had zero tolerance for all the Jewish mothers in our town and wanted to avoid them at all costs. If there was a parents' night or a teacher conference, it was understood early on that our mother would rather set herself on fire; we were lucky if she showed up at our bat mitzvah. Unfortunately, my father loved any sort of school event and would usually show up hooting and hollering in the front row, wearing snow boots and a sweater covered in dog hair.

Normally, I would have expected my mother to knock on the basement door and explain to us how to avoid getting smacked, but who knew what kind of high she was on after her nude pep rally upstairs.

"I heard that men fall asleep after they have sex," Sloane offered.

"Dad didn't look tired when he was chasing me with his belt," I told her.

"I don't know if I can wait for Mom to come for us. I'm really hungry."

I climbed up on the dryer and took a seat. "Mom was wearing a nurse's hat."

"What?" She seemed concerned.

"When I walked in on them, she was naked and Dad was chasing her on the bed. I saw his penis."

"Ew…"

"Ew? Ew? You're the pervert who made me do it!"

"I didn't think you'd really do it," she said.

"You knew I would!"

This was so typical of Sloane. She always backed out of a situation once controversy found its way into it. My brothers and sisters knew they could get me to do anything, mostly because I wanted them to like me, but Sloane was a different story. I wasn't sure I liked her.

"You are so double-faced," I told her. "I hate you."

"It's 'two-faced,' dummy, and I am not!" she said.

"Oh, really, what about the time with the Feinstein sisters," I reminded her.

A year earlier when I was in kindergarten and she was in the fifth grade, we would walk to school together in the morning. One day, two other sisters were on their way to school with their five-foot-tall Irish wolfhound following closely behind. They were telling their dog to go back home but the dog wouldn't listen. Sloane was scared because the dog was so big and kept growling at us. The girls were laughing at my sister for being scared of their dog, but in reality, this dog was scary. He was huge and mean and looked like he belonged in a wild animal park. He had a large open wound on his hind leg and looked as if he were slowly decomposing.

"Stop laughing at my sister, you dumb girls," I yelled. "Your dog is ugly and belongs in a shelter."

"Shut up," Sloane said through her teeth. "Shut up."

"Oh, look, Sloane needs her six-year-old sister to defend her," one of the girls sneered.

"No, she doesn't," I yelled, then turned to Sloane for some backup—only to see her running furiously in the direction of the school.

Years later I learned the word "turncoat" in history class. Had I had this kind of ammunition against her earlier, things might have ended up differently.

"I dropped the camera in Mom's room," I told her.

"Oh, that's just great." She stood up with her hands on her hips. "I have pictures on there of Marsha's sleepover party. We all took our pajamas off and took pictures while playing Truth or Dare."

"Why?" I asked.

"Because. We felt like it."

"I'm telling," I told her.

"Who cares?" she said. "It was only girls."

"Lesbian!" I yelled.

I knew what a lesbian was because my father's best friend from high school's wife left him for another woman and my father referred to her only as "the lesbian."

"I am not a lesbian. Shut up!"

"Yes, you are. I knew it."

"If anyone's a lesbian, it's you," she said. That shut me up.

"It's better for us just to go upstairs and get it over with," she said. "At least then we can eat something. I want a sandwich."

"How can you think about food at a time like this?" I asked her. "Do you think people at the Battle of Gettysburg had time for peanut butter and jelly?"

Switching tactics, she reminded me that it was a Thursday night and we would be missing *The Cosby Show* if we stayed in the basement. That would have been enough to drive any level-headed seven-year-old insane.

Even so, I was ready to stay in the basement as long as it took for my dad to forget about what had happened. I had seen his penis and did not think I would be able to look him in the eye any time soon.

I thought about escaping through our one basement window, but then I would only be outside and it was cold. Winter was not a good time to run away from home, especially without an overnight bag.

I wondered if my mother was actually mad at me too. I told my sister I would need more than the five dollars we had originally agreed on.

"No way! You got caught. That was not part of the deal! I'm not even sure I'm going to give you the five dollars!"

I smacked her on the back of the head. She tried to hit me, but I ducked. Then she ran toward the stairs.

"No! Don't go!!!" I yelled, but she was already up the stairs and out the door when I ran up after her to try and pull her back down.

I locked the door just as I heard her get another smack, but this one sounded like it was on her face. I listened as she started wailing. This upset me deeply. I wanted her to be a strong gladiator type, the kind of girl I envisioned myself at thirteen. A weight lifter with a steadfast disposition and a designer wardrobe. But she was a sissy, and I could not follow suit.

It was becoming clear to me that the only way out of this was to turn the tables on my father. Instead of running, I would never leave the basement. Not even if he begged me. I would tell him how sickened I was by what I saw and that I now had reservations about going out into the real world without a psychiatrist by my side. I would insist on therapy two to three times a week and also insist that it take place during school hours. I would demand an entirely new wardrobe and that they allow me to move into the master bedroom, while my parents took my room. I would make them beg for my forgiveness while threatening them with lawsuits: unfit parenting, involving a minor in sexual activities, pornographic exposure to a minor, the list would go on and on. I saw *Irreconcilable Differences*. I was no dummy.

My father knocked on the door for the last time that night. "Are you ready to come out and get your smack?"

"I want Mom," I said. There was no response from the other side of the door. I wondered how Sloane's sandwich tasted with her bloody lip. I wondered if the Huxtable children had ever walked in on their parents having sex. It was important to occupy my mind with other thoughts, so I decided to do some laundry. Maybe when my mother came and saw that all the laundry had been done she would tell my father, who would come to the conclusion that I wasn't such a bad kid after all. I took one look at the laundry machine with all its buttons and dials and decided sleep was more appealing.

I woke up sometime in the middle of the night after feeling something crawl over my foot. I jumped up and ran to the top of the stairs. Slowly, I opened the door. All the lights were out. No one was in sight. I went straight to bed and fell asleep.

My father came in my room at seven a.m. to wake me up. "It's time to get up, love." Then he walked downstairs.

I was ecstatic. Sloane should have listened to me the whole time! I got dressed for school, had a bowl of Lucky Charms in celebration of my personal victory, and brushed my teeth.

My father said he'd be outside warming up the car. You never knew which car this was because we had about ten in our driveway. My father fancied himself a used car dealer, but as I understood it, "dealing" meant buying and then selling. Cars would pile up in our driveway for years at a time, and on most mornings my father would have to jump-start one or more to get us to school. Each car was more embarrassing than the next and none were made in the decade in which we lived.

I went outside and jumped into the car that was smoking, which was a fluorescent turquoise Plymouth something or other with vinyl interior. I was flying so high from my victory, I decided to compliment him on the car.

"I love this color, Dad."

My firm yet supple seven-year-old ass had hardly touched the vinyl when my own father sucker-slapped me. Right on my nose. I was in pure, titillated horror. I couldn't even respond with words. I thought for sure my nose was broken, but then the tingling sensation died—just when I was starting to enjoy it.

"You thought you were gonna get away without a smack, didn't you?" he said.

I instantly broke down and cried like a little girl. I knew, of course, that I was a little girl, but I did not like acting like one. And I was both hurt and angry at having to drive to school with someone who just smacked me. I felt like such a moron for thinking I could outsmart my father with some lame compliment about his piece-of-shit car. This was definitely a feeling I didn't like then, or the hundreds of times I've felt it since.

I didn't say anything the whole ride. When we reached the school, I got out and slammed the door. He drove away with some sort of car part scraping the sidewalk, possibly the muffler.

Now when I look back at that experience, I realize that maybe walking in on my parents in all their glory was what led me to embrace my own sexuality. The way those two were enjoying themselves made me realize there was more to life than macaroni and cheese and *The Brady Bunch*. I wanted in on that action and didn't appreciate having to wait another ten years to get the real party started.

I wiped my tears, picked off a Lucky Charm that was stuck to my skirt, tried to recapture some semblance of dignity, and headed inside the school.

Obviously, I would need to tell all the first graders about seeing my parents have sex.

The Beginning of the End

MANY PEOPLE FEEL like a one-night stand is something to be ashamed of or embarrassed by. I disagree. There are many ways to get to know someone, and my personal favorite is seeing them naked in Happy Baby pose.

I also feel it is important to have sex soon after meeting someone in order to find out if you have sexual chemistry together. Otherwise, you could wait two to three months after you start dating someone only to discover that your new boyfriend is bad in bed, or even worse, is into anal beads and duct tape.

I can remember my first one-night stand like it was yesterday. Well, maybe not the first. Or the second...or the fifth. I'll just begin with what I can remember and not concern myself with order.

It was a starry summer night at the Jersey shore. Picture violins and a harmonica. Now picture the harmonica up my ass. I think it's safe to say that the Jersey shore, specifically an area called Belmar, isn't what pops into mind when thinking of romance.

I was around eighteen at the time. It's hard to say since I started lying about my age as soon as I got my boobs.

My girlfriend Ivory and I had just graduated from high school and decided to celebrate by the water. Ivory and I had met freshman year and had been close ever since. Her parents came to America from Cuba long before Ivory was born. They had since tried to prove their loyalty to America with every child they'd had. Her brother's name is Cincinnati and she has a sister named July, presumably after the fourth. Somewhere along the way, they also converted to Judaism.

We were discovering the Jersey shore for the first time and felt it was our duty as Jersey girls to really pay our respects to the Garden State. We were tired of sleeping around with the average Joe, Dick, and Harry. A challenge was in order.

We were in the mood for dancing, so we found a loud, dark bar with music pouring out of it. I had her pick out the hottest guy in the bar and I fearlessly approached him. It was very empowering to go up to a babe like him and be received so well. I thought, Wow, I must be really good-looking. Until I started dancing.

I don't know if you've ever seen a Jewish girl who's been self-diagnosed as tone-deaf cut a rug on a Jersey shore dance floor before, but it definitely resembles someone whose motor skills haven't fully developed. In my state of drunkenness, I was fueled by delusions of being an original cast member of the play *Chicago*. I decided to do the number where I rub my ass into my partner's crotch while my arms grab his neck behind me. When in doubt, ladies, this move will always guarantee you at least a slice of pizza.

I decided on two slices instead of one; I'd burned a

number of calories during my *Flashdance* number and wanted to reassure my guy that I wasn't one of those girls who didn't eat. We had a great time eating and watching my best friend Ivory make out with her score for the night. Her guy was a real piece of Jersey trash, and they ended up tearing off in his banana yellow Camaro. I went back to my guy's house and proceeded to have some of the best sex I can barely remember.

What I do recall is turning his ceiling fan on "high" (there are two things in this world I cannot sleep without: a fan and a silk set of eye shades), ripping his clothes off, and looking at one of the finest bodies that our ecosystem has ever created. The next morning I was walking with a considerable limp and wasn't able to deduce if this was a result of the dancing or the sex. After catching a glimpse of my hair in the mirror, I considered scheduling an audition for the lead in *The Lion King*.

I dated this beautiful hunk of flesh for the next eight months. His looks overrode his personality for the first couple of months, but after a while it became harder and harder to ignore. We would go out to dinner, and the minute he was done eating, he'd put his fork down and ask for the check. The summerhouse he rented with four other guys had hot water for only the first ten minutes and then it would become freezing, so he insisted on taking showers before me, because I was his little "trouper." This was also someone who wouldn't let me borrow his toothbrush on an occasion when I forgot my own, for fear of mouth germs. I liked his roommates better than him, so I would hang out with them during the day and then go up and have sex with him at night. I'd turn up the music loud so we wouldn't be tempted to talk.

Our relationship finally ended when he took to waking me up in the wee hours of the morning when he would go surfing. He thought it might be fun to have me come and watch. "Fun for who?" I wanted to ask. I had never asked him to come to happy hour and watch me drink. I gently explained to him that I would rather sit at home and staple my hand to a wall than watch someone wearing a wet suit wipe out every thirty seconds. Besides, my ass didn't look so good in a bikini after a summer of margaritas, and I thought it was time I found someone farther inland.

I realized that summer that a one-night stand is called just that because it should only be for one night.

DUMB AND DUMBER

ONE SUMMER, MY girlfriend Ivory and I decided that after all our hard partying at community college, we deserved a vacation. My parents' summer home in Martha's Vineyard would be empty until mid-July, so Ivory and I generously volunteered to look after things.

We had many rules that summer. After a long conversation about money and responsibility, we both agreed that a job would add too much pressure to our very hectic drinking schedule. At one point during that summer, when we were really broke, we were left with no choice but to join a cleaning service. It only took fifteen minutes of scrubbing the inside of a toilet for me to realize that the only time I felt comfortable facedown in one was after a hard night of margaritas. It was then that we resolved it should be men's responsibility to pay for our alcohol and whatever small amount of food was required.

Our other rules were that we were both required to lie in the sun with nothing higher than an SPF 2 and for no fewer than three hours per day. I explained to Ivory that you could get better color while actually in the ocean, but even with Cuban parents Ivory had never learned to swim.

I wasn't a good enough swimmer to teach her, so instead, I bought her a pair of yellow water wings.

Ivory and I had taken enough pot to the Vineyard to last us through the end of the month. I fancied myself quite the pothead. We ended up getting so high on the drive up, however, that we rolled each and every morsel of it into finely rolled joints, then proceeded to smoke our entire supply the first night on the island. I had a similar experience with macaroni and cheese once. I haven't had either since.

One of the more enjoyable rules we came up with that summer was to photograph our victims of sexual abuse. We took pictures with every guy we brought back to the house.

One night we were at a bar playing pool with two guys. Ivory and I were on the same team and hadn't shot a single ball into a pocket when I picked one up and stuffed it in a side hole. The guys took my lead, and it turned into a game of handball with all of us throwing balls in every direction we saw a pocket. Unfortunately, I don't have the best hand-eye coordination, and in an attempt to corner pocket one of the balls, I sent it reeling over the pool table straight into the wall behind it, where it stayed. Shortly after, the bartender asked us to leave.

We took our cue and went back to my parents', got wrecked, then took our men to our respective love lairs. As I was rolling around in the bed I was probably conceived in, I ripped off my guy's T-shirt to discover a completely hairless chest. Since there were no burn scars, I had to assume that this young man had done this to himself voluntarily. There was no hair anywhere on his body. Not in his pants or on his legs.

"Where's your hair?" I asked him.

"I shave," he told me.

"On purpose?"

I was instantly nauseous and may have thrown up a little, which ended up working to my advantage in orchestrating my escape.

"Are you okay?" he said.

I blushed and said that this had been my very first night of drinking. "I guess alcohol is not really my thing," I lied.

He said it was okay and maybe I'd feel better in the morning.

"Maybe," I said, "but you won't be around to find out."

Unfortunately, I had to break up Ivory's party in order for her to drive my guy home. She wasn't thrilled, but it turns out her guy was missing a few hairs too. The ones on his head. As they were rolling around on her bed, his toupee came flying off and landed on the curling iron that was left on for what could very well have been the entire summer. Ivory liked older men, but not old enough to have no hair. Apparently, this guy really got the short end of the stick in the looks department. How he did in the other stick departments, we would never know.

Later on that summer, I started fooling around with a guy named Turtle. This was to become a common theme of mine—dating men nicknamed after animals. Later on there was Chicken, and for a brief two-week absence of mind, there was a boy named Rooster. Chicken got his name because he could outrun anyone, and Rooster got his because he got up every morning at the crack of dawn. Needless to say, my relationship with Rooster didn't make it past our first sleepover. Chicken and Rooster were not related.

I liked Turtle. I had met him when I stopped at the gas station where he worked. There was only one bathroom, and as I was leaning down to cover the seat with toilet paper, with my pants around my ankles, the door flew open.

"Whoa! Sorry about that," he apologized hastily as he shut the door.

When I walked out he was waiting next to the door with an embarrassed look on his face.

"That's not really my best angle," I told him.

Both our faces were red with embarrassment and we started laughing uncontrollably. To the point where I had to use the bathroom again.

"Did you leave me any toilet paper?" he asked as I came out of the bathroom the second time.

"Yeah, there's a little left on the seat."

Turtle and I got along great. He was the type of blue-collar alcoholic that you could have a really solid fling with. Turtle was more laid-back than the Dalai Lama. He was the perfect prototype for a summer fling: a cute, flirty island boy, but not the type you'd miss in the fall. He fixed bikes at the gas station for the summer, and he definitely didn't go to college. He had a vocabulary that could battle my six-year-old nephew's.

Turtle had an uncle named Marty whom Ivory immediately took a shine to. He owned his very own gas station, and Ivory *loved* the smell of gas.

So there we were, two middle-class Jewish girls from

Jersey hangin' tough at the gas station where our paramours worked. Our parents would have been so proud. We'd go by there from the beach for about a month straight, refill Ivory's water wings at the air pump, and watch our men fix cars, Joey Buttafucco–style. We'd sit around sipping our Mike's Hard Lemonade waiting for the boys to finish working so we could head out to some dive bar that accepted fake IDs. We each had our favorite pair of cutoff Levi's that we wore low on our hips and ripped up the sides. Sometimes we wore a shirt, but if we skipped eating that day, we'd also skip wearing shirts and just sport our bikini tops.

"This is like the prime of our life," Ivory said to me one day as we watched our men work and I had just finished pumping a customer's gas.

"Yeah." I smiled as I lit up a Marlboro Red. "It really doesn't get any better than this."

Marty and Ivory got into a big fight one night at a bar that had a lot of wood chips on the floor. He made a comment to her about not drinking anymore and she started screaming, "Oh, so now I'm an alcoholic, is that it?" Marty was mostly soft-spoken, but I think he and his liver had just had enough. The four of us had been hanging out for a month straight, every night.

Being the supportive friend I was, I decided to storm out with her. Unfortunately, I lost my footing, ended up sliding out the door, and got a splinter right below my right butt cheek. I fall a lot, but other than that I can pretty much control my liquor. Ivory's the kind of girl who gets drunk and immediately starts slurring. I have a lot of friends like that, and I think it's because it makes me look "more together."

The next morning Ivory told me she wanted to go to an Alcoholics Anonymous meeting. Great, I thought. Just what I needed. The summer was going so well. I had to sit down and explain to her that AA was for quitters, and that "alcoholic" was one ugly word. You spend one night in women's prison, and all of a sudden people want to label you! I told her I didn't think she had a drinking problem, and besides, they don't have AA in Martha's Vineyard. After all, it was an island. Any normal person wouldn't have believed me, but Ivory loved hearing me lie, especially when it meant she didn't have to do something she wouldn't be good at anyway.

Marty called the next day to apologize, for what I don't know. This happened with all of her boyfriends. They would somehow convince themselves overnight that they were the ones who were wrong. It was too late, though. Once Ivory made her mind up about a guy there was no turning back. She never whined or complained after a breakup; she just moved forward. She had just come back from her morning jog where she met her new boyfriend, deciding we were done with the whole "blue-collar" thing. I was fine with that because I was getting tired of hearing myself scream the name Turtle in bed.

"We're moving on to Latin America," she told me.

"*Salud,*" I said, holding up a glass of Slim-Fast. "Finally, we can get back to your roots."

Her new boyfriend, Jorge, didn't speak a word of English, and luckily enough, he had a friend who didn't either. Beautiful Latin boys. They were our sophisticated Latin lovers, who would cook for us at my parents' house for the next two weeks. They introduced us to salsa, sangria, and communication via the *ojos*.

My guy's name was Hector, which he pronounced "Heeeeector." We couldn't really communicate, but he seemed nice, and he was a good swimmer. We would make out for hours at a time, but that's as far as it went. The one time he tried to initiate sex, we were in the shower. I was on the edge of the tub where there's a little area to sit, and he grabbed my hands to bring me closer to him. As I got up, my feet slipped out from underneath me and I went flying through his legs, landing on my back and hitting my head. The last thing I had tried to grab onto for balance was his penis. After that, we decided to keep things more casual.

Jorge, on the other hand, really fell for Ivory and actually proposed marriage to her. She had this thing where guys would propose to her all the time, which I never understood. Every guy she dated was absolutely in love with her. I mean, Ivory was very attractive and funny, but men acted like her vagina had some sort of potpourri shooting out of it.

Anyway, Jorge proposed and Ivory accepted like she always did until she sobered up and realized Jorge probably just wanted his visa.

The next day we received a phone call from the Martha's Vineyard Police Department wanting to know if we had any idea of the whereabouts of a Mr. Jorge Menendez, who was wanted for grand theft auto. No wonder they were cooking for us at home.

I told the police my parents weren't home and our gardener's name was Alejandro. Other than that, I didn't know anyone of Spanish descent.

I explained to Ivory that our summer of love was over and we needed to vacate the premises. We packed our bags, called home, and told our parents that we were homesick. That's slang for "on the run."

We discussed our future and decided since we were both twenty and hated college as well as New Jersey, it was time to broaden our horizons.

"How does California sound to you?" Ivory asked. "You could be an actress and I'll get a real job."

"Finally," I moaned. "Now you're starting to make sense."

And off we went.

GUESS WHO'S LEAVING THROUGH THE WINDOW?

"SHVARTZER" is the term my father uses to refer to black people. It is a Yiddish slang word that basically means "black," "colored," or "Negro." My father will argue with you until the sun comes up that he doesn't have a racist bone in his body, one of his favorite defenses being, "Are you kidding? I love the blacks, they make great employees. Plus, they can run like *hell*." This is the same man who went to a cocktail party in the late eighties with my mother and upon seeing the only black couple there, approached the woman and asked her if she would be interested in cleaning our house.

I met my first black boyfriend at the local community college. Tyrone and I sat next to each other in Russian history class. Our professor was a thick-accented Russian who talked more about his childhood than he did about Russia's history. On our midterms we were asked actual questions about his personal life—in what city he was born, how old was he when he learned to ride a bike without training wheels. Tyrone and I would laugh at the absurdity of Professor Beregova's self-importance, but everyone else there seemed to think this was perfectly normal lesson planning.

"This can't be happening at real colleges," Tyrone said to me one day after class. "Why doesn't anyone else in class think this is strange?"

"I know," I said. "And this is supposed to be one of the top-ten community colleges in the country."

When I brought Tyrone home for dinner, my father tried as hard as he could to act like it didn't bother him but was constantly looking at Tyrone out of the corner of his eye. When we held hands, my father twitched slightly and looked away. I had fantasies of inviting him to sleep over, knowing my father wouldn't object in front of Tyrone. If it had been a white boyfriend, my father would have protested in front of everyone, but in his never-ending plea to appear color-blind, I knew my dad would not only allow him to sleep over but would probably offer up his own pajamas. The only topics my father was able to discuss with Tyrone were football, basketball, and slavery.

Tyrone and I broke up a few months later when he transferred to a more respectable college somewhere in Michigan. When I told my father about his transfer, he feigned disappointment. "That's too bad, love. He was a nice guy. Not too dark, could almost pass for a Colombian."

"Why would he want to pass for a Colombian, Dad?" I asked.

"Listen, don't start with the racial stuff, okay? I think the *shvartzers* have a lot of courage; I love the blacks. Dogs don't seem to like them, but I don't have a problem. Look at Oprah!"

"That's real nice, Dad. You have a real way with words. You should think about running for public office."

"Yeah, well I'll tell ya, it wouldn't be the worst thing. You're not the first person to tell me that, love. And you probably won't be the last."

Tyrone had been the first black man I had had sex with, and I felt very strongly about venturing further into that arena. So during the two months I had to kill before Ivory and I were off to California, I started chatting online with Jerome, whom I met on ChocolateSingles.us. Since he also lived with his parents, I had to wait until mine were out of town before we could set up our first rendezvous. My brothers and sisters had all moved out and I was the only child left at home. Jerome and I had exchanged photos of ourselves, and as long as he looked somewhat similar to his picture, I knew we would be having sex.

We agreed on dinner and a movie, which I suggested mostly because I didn't want to be obvious about my over-whelming desire to have sex with another black man.

We planned to meet at six o'clock at a steakhouse not far from my parents' house. Unfortunately, earlier that day I had done quite a number on my hair. I had been inspired to cut my own bangs—the result of which was not at all posi-tive. In short, I looked as if I had lost a fight with a pair of craft scissors. I managed to get my bangs under control by placing a barrette directly above my forehead where it met my hairline. It wasn't a good look for anyone, but on the bright side, the severity with which my bangs were pulled back made me look much more alert than usual.

Jerome was already seated when I arrived. He was six-two and gorgeous, with a body absolutely to die for. He was twenty-five, had a short buzz cut, light brown eyes, and a big happy smile. He was ten times better looking than his picture. "Jerome?" I asked innocently, as if he weren't the only black person in the entire place.

"Hello," he said, standing up to give me a kiss on the cheek. His skin was the softest I had ever felt, and it was the exact color of a Reese's Peanut Butter Cup. I couldn't believe how beautiful he was. If this guy hadn't lived with his parents, he would've been out of my league. He glanced at my barrette a couple of times and I felt my face getting hotter. He was obviously wondering why I'd placed a barrette so close to my forehead.

I was furious about giving myself a home haircut. How could I have been so stupid? Clearly, I had to say something to allay his fears. "I had a little accident today," I told him.

"Oh, no," he said.

"It was nothing serious. I was actually volunteering at the Boys and Girls Club of America and a little boy set my hair on fire by accident. He has ADD and it's a pretty sad story."

"Oh, my God, were you hurt?" Jerome asked.

"No, no, no," I said, relieved that the lie seemed to be working. "I felt pretty stupid when I looked in the mirror, but I was more concerned about Linus."

"How old is the boy?" asked a horrified Jerome.

I scrambled to think of an appropriate age for a child who would set someone else on fire. "He's seven," I told him, "but challenged." I didn't know where these lies were coming from, but I couldn't stop myself. I was so intimidated by him I just jumped into a story I was sure would give us a lot to talk about.

Within the next fifteen minutes Linus had also been born a Siamese twin whose brother didn't make it through the surgery and whose biological mother had tried to auction him off on eBay.

"I didn't even know there was a Boys and Girls Club around here," said Jerome.

I had never seen a Boys & Girls Club in my life but wasn't about to tell Jerome that. "Oh, there's one at the mall," I blurted.

"Really?" he asked. "That's weird."

"It's new," I said. I knew I would have to stop lying eventually but didn't know how to. We needed to change the subject quickly and I needed a drink to relax.

Though I wasn't of legal drinking age, I had an ID with my picture on it and all of Sloane's information. My mother had given me Sloane's birth certificate when I turned eighteen after I explained how difficult it would be to fit in at community college without an ID. My mother agreed to aid my abuse of alcohol but only if I promised never to tell my newly converted Mormon sister, whose identity I had stolen.

"Are you okay? You look—" Jerome said.

"I'm fine," I said.

If I could just calm down for a minute, I could be normal. I hailed the waiter and ordered a vodka and cranberry. Jerome ordered an ice water. Shit, I thought.

"You don't want a drink?" I asked.

"I don't drink," Jerome said.

This was going to be a complete disaster. What did he mean he didn't drink?

"Ever?" I pressed on.

"I just don't like the taste," he told me. Then he leaned in. "That doesn't mean I don't know how to have a good time."

I smiled and said, "Are you sure you don't want to have just a beer or something?"

"I'm sure." He smiled. This was going to be a long dinner. I had never been on a date with someone who didn't drink and I didn't like it.

If this guy had any sort of affiliation with Alcoholics Anonymous, he would definitely try to recruit me, so I asked to make sure.

"You're not in AA, are you?" I said it in a way that implied if he was in AA and would be bothered by my drinking, I would simply skip it. This wasn't really going to happen, of course; I just wanted to come off like I had manners. I immediately had images of becoming his AA sponsor and waiting for the night he'd call me and tell me he wanted a drink. I'd be jumping up and down screaming through the phone, "I have one! Come over!"

"No, no. You go ahead, I don't mind. I just don't like it."

So I went full speed ahead. By my fifth drink, I was beginning to be the more normal version of myself, which meant that I would only pepper my stories with half-truths rather than create them entirely out of thin air.

It turned out that he was a third-year law student at Seton Hall. His mother and father owned a shoe store outlet in Secaucus, New Jersey.

"Oh, wow. I love shoes," was my soulful response.

He was a really decent guy with a charming personality

and I had no idea at all what he was doing with me. He loved his parents a lot and talked about his mother in a way that more men should. It was sweet to watch and I hoped that when we married, he would hold me in the same regard.

The thought of not sleeping with him right away crossed my mind, because I wanted his respect, but there was no way I would be able to control myself. He was too cute and sweet. And I knew if I dated him, he would probably end up hating me anyway.

"Do you want to skip the movie?" I asked.

"Sure, if you want to," he replied.

"My parents are out of town. We could go back to my house and hang out."

"We could do that," he said.

He followed me back to my house and parked his car in the street. Like most first-time visitors, he asked me why there were so many cars in our driveway and I explained to him that my father had a bad car habit and was unable to sell any of the jalopies sitting in our driveway. I told him if he wanted, I could get him a sweet deal on an '85 Buick wagon with no engine.

"So none of these cars work?" he asked.

"A couple of them," I told him. "It's not like you'd want to drive them anywhere anyway."

He had the same scowl on his face that our neighbor had every time he called the police to report my father for having too many cars in the driveway.

"Jeez," Jerome said.

We got inside and went straight into the den. I turned on

the television and poured myself a Grey Goose and Tang. He, of course, wanted nothing alcoholic, so I gave him a Coke. It felt like I was at a Chuck E. Cheese birthday party. How was he going to make his move on me without any alcohol? I could easily make a move on him but wasn't sure if he liked me as much as I liked his body.

It was only nine o'clock, so we turned on the TV and started watching *America's Funniest Home Videos*. I was tempted to pop in the porno I had stolen from my brother but didn't want Jerome to think I was completely fucked up. My brother was in culinary school and had left behind more than fifty porno videos that he went to the trouble of hiding in the linen closet. Every once in a while he would call home and ask my mom to send him one of his videos. They weren't in their jackets anymore, so you would know they were pornos only by their titles. My mother asked me once if I had ever seen *Kristen Does Kentucky,* and I told her, "Yes, it's a story about a girl who is torn between two lovers. Literally."

"Your brother must really like it, he wants me to send it to him," she said.

Jerome and I started moving closer and closer together. He was rubbing his hand back and forth on my leg when I threw my head in his lap and stared up at him.

"You're adorable," I told him.

He laughed and then kissed me. Finally, we were making out. He had the softest lips I had ever felt and he smelled like Drakkar. I loved, loved, loved Drakkar. I put my hands around his back and held on to his immense linebackerlike physique. Everywhere I put my hand, I found a new muscle.

I put my hands inside his shirt to find the hardest six-pack I had ever felt. This guy was in unbelievable shape, and his skin was sooooo soft.

I was so turned on I could barely control myself. I had to stay cool, though, and not forget to suck in my stomach. I wanted him to think I was on a physical par with him, so I kept my body in its most flattering position: horizontal.

He maneuvered himself to get on top of me and do some dry-humping when I felt what could only be a third leg. I wiggled underneath him in order to confirm.

"Is that your penis?" I gasped.

He let out a small chuckle and kept on kissing me.

"Seriously," I said. "Is that your penis?"

He stopped kissing me and lifted his head to look sternly at me. "Yes, that's my penis."

"Well, that's gonna be a big problem," I said.

He just stared at me.

"I'm sorry," I told him. "Your penis is too big." I had a girlfriend who had cried during sex once and now I knew why.

He got up off of me. "We can still fool around," I assured him. "We just can't have sex."

"Well, what makes you think I want to have sex with you anyway?" he snapped.

I wanted to tell him that it was pretty obvious, judging from the time bomb growing in his pants.

"All right, geez, don't get so offended," I said. "Just in case you wanted to, I want you to know I can't." You would have had to be the size of the Lincoln Tunnel to accommodate that thing.

"Well, you're not the first one," he said, defeated. Apparently this had happened before.

"Really? I'm so sorry, you're just too big. It's like a space shuttle," I told him. He looked bummed and I felt bad for him. "We can go in my room and do other things." By other things I meant sleep, because I didn't want that thing coming out of its shell for fear that it might attack.

Once we got into my room we did a lot of kissing and heavy petting, and that was pretty much it. We started dry-humping, and I was pretty sure he came in his pants because he passed out about thirty seconds later.

At around eight the next morning I heard sounds coming from the kitchen. My room was on the first floor not far away.

It was my father talking to our dog, Whitefoot. "Are you a good Jewish doggy who was a good little boy the whole ride home? Are you? Do you want to go to Hebrew school with all the other Jewish doggies in the neighborhood? Are you a good boy? Are you a good boy? Are you a good boy?"

Fuck. My parents were home. I looked over at Jerome, who was sound asleep. I quickly got up and locked my door, then reconsidered, put on some clothes, and woke him up. "Jerome," I whispered, "my parents are home."

"Oh, shit!" he said, flinging himself out of bed. "I thought they were in Martha's Vineyard."

"They were. I don't know what they're doing back so soon. Just stay here and I'll find out if they're leaving again."

In order for Jerome to leave through the front door he would have to pass through the kitchen. Things didn't look good. I opened the door and strolled out.

"There she is! Hi, love, what's cookin'?" My dad was in a good mood, and I wanted it to stay that way.

"What are you doing home?" I asked sleepily, as if I wasn't totally awake and alert.

"We met a couple up at the Vineyard who need a car for their son. He's going off to college. I told them I was a car dealer and they want to buy a car. I'm bringing one back up for them. That neat little Civic we've got out in the driveway." He said this as if I hadn't seen the two-door blue hatchback with one of the doors covered in red primer every time I pulled up to the house. He also said it like it was a great car that anyone in his right mind would want to buy. "Those little cars last forever," he said.

"Does it even start?" I asked him.

"Does it even start? Of course it does! It just needs a little help, that's all. I'm gonna go get the oil changed and then drive back up today."

"Good fucking luck" is what I wanted to say. "Is Mom still on the Vineyard?" is what I really said.

"Yes, she is, doll, and she misses you terribly. That's why you can drive your car up so we have a ride home."

"When?" I asked, but before he could answer, there was a loud bang on the front porch outside. I have never spoken to Kato Kaelin, but I'm assuming it was similar to the loud bang he heard when O.J. snuck back in the house after killing Nicole and Ron (or not).

"What in the hell was that?" my dad asked, as Whitefoot spit out his bagel with cream cheese, started barking, and ran to the front door.

"I didn't hear anything, Dad."

"Don't be an idiot, love, of course you did," he said as he got up to go to the front door. I walked behind him, trying to think of a way to keep him from seeing what I could only presume was Jerome making a getaway. But I couldn't think of anything.

As my father opened the door we saw Jerome topless and running down our front lawn. He leaped into his car and drove away.

"What in the hell was that?" my father asked.

I just stared at the sky, hoping for an incoming asteroid.

"Goddamn it, Chelsea. What in the hell have you done now?"

My relationship with my father had been on the proverbial fritz since the time I was fifteen and called the police to report him for child molesting. He had never molested me, but I wanted to have a party that weekend and needed him out of the house. It had been a long time since he had smacked me in the face, his signature move, but I was still nervous. Only a couple months prior he had gone into what I can only describe as a King Kong/Donkey Kong fit of rage where he unloaded all the planters on our back deck, along with their flowers, plants, and soil, onto the ground. This was in response to my mother hiding the remote control for the television and my father being too lazy to get up and turn it on manually.

I backed away from him as quickly as I could and made a run for my room. "You're a real piece of work, you know that, Chelsea. A real piece of work. I have a good mind to call the police and report the car he was driving. I'm sure it was stolen," my father shouted, following me.

"No, Dad," I said, behind my closed door. "It wasn't stolen, you racist. It was his."

"Goddamn it, Chelsea, open this goddamned door before I break it in. What kind of girl runs around town with a bunch of strangers?" he yelled. "Do you even know that guy?"

"Of course I do," I argued from behind my door. "We met on the Internet."

"Oh, for Christ's sake. You know what, Chelsea, I've got news for you. If you want people to show you respect, you don't just *give* your shit away."

Huh? Was my dad suggesting that I start charging people?

I considered telling my father that Jerome's penis was too big and we didn't have sex, but I didn't know if the word "penis" was allowed. I knew "slut" was because he had just called me that. I looked over and saw my open window and then saw my father's face come through it.

"Aaaah!" I screamed.

"You better listen to me, you little pain in the ass!" My father's head is the size of a beach ball and couldn't fit through the window with a shoehorn, but it didn't stop him from trying. "Your mother and I are sick of your shit, running around with strange men, your half-assed attempt at community college, no job. What the hell kind of life do you want for yourself?" As my father was yelling out one insult after another, I thought about throwing a snow globe at his head. Unfortunately, I didn't have one.

"Get your stuff together. We're leaving in two hours for the Vineyard and you need to follow me in case the Civic breaks down." Then he turned and walked back into the house.

About two and a half hours into the ride, my father's car got a flat tire. I pulled up behind him and watched him try to fix it. Moments later, a Toyota 4Runner stopped by the side of the road and a black man got out. I climbed out of my car as well. We both met at my father's car, and the stranger asked, "Do you need help with that flat tire, sir?"

My father looked up and said, "Yes, that would be nice. Don't know what happened here. I just need to get the spare on so I can have this tire looked at." The tire needed to be thrown in the trash, not "looked at," but this was another case of my father being delusional about the condition of his cars. When my father noticed me checking out the black guy, who wasn't half bad looking, he said, "Chelsea, get back in your car and keep your pants on." The black man glanced at both of us with a confused expression on his face and then kneeled down to start loosening the bolts.

Once we got to the Vineyard, my father gave my mother the rundown of what had taken place.

"Whitefoot and I are having breakfast at the table, and who do you think pops out of her room like everything's coming up roses? Chelsea, that's who. And before you know it, I hear the *shvartzer* jump out of her window and steal a car."

"Dad, shut up. You know he didn't steal that car, it was his," I said. I was bored by the replay of events.

My mother came over and sat down beside me. "Melvin, please leave her alone," she said.

"Oh, here we go. Mommy loves Chelsea and Daddy is the bad guy. I'm always the fall guy. I get it, I see what's happening here. It's daddy-bashing time, is that it? I'm the worst daddy in the whole wide world!"

I wanted this whole discussion to be over with already. But mostly I wanted my father to stop referring to himself as Daddy. It was creeping me out. My brother Greg walked in as all this was going on and gave me a high five.

"Good work, Chels. Nicely done."

"Don't encourage her, Greg. Chelsea, you need to get prioritized, not parade around doing nothing all day but watching your programs and talking on the goddamned telephone. And what the hell is it about the blacks that you like so much? Are you just trying to piss me off?" he asked.

"Well, they are known to have rather large penises," Greg said.

I was out the door before I could see my father's face explode with wild fury. My brother and mother weren't far behind, and the three of us jumped into Greg's car and headed into town for some ice cream.

After two days of complete silence from my father, he ventured out and got three large cases of blueberries. Blueberries are my favorite. He left them on the counter and drove back to New Jersey.

MY LITTLE NUGGET

I THINK WE can all agree that sleeping around is a great way to meet people. Furthermore, sleeping around with midgets is a great way to meet midgets.

The great thing about sleeping with a midget is that first you get to have sex with them and then you can use them as a pillow. Those little midgets have it so easy. Sometimes when I see one, I want to chase it. I don't want to scare them, but I want to hold them and cuddle them. Mostly I would like one for the carpool lane.

I guess what I'm trying to say is this: If you want something bad enough, you just have to go after it.

This is what I can remember. I showed up at a party in Cabo San Lucas, Mexico. I had been living in California for more than a year, with Ivory, and I was meeting my sisters for a vacation, but they weren't arriving until the next night. A hotel room all to myself is my idea of a good time.

I went to the pool, where I met a couple who told me they were going to some sort of Cinco de Mayoish party with plenty of margaritas. I thought it sounded like a great idea, and my new friends and I decided to go.

It's always the couples who are the friendliest who have

the most problems. It makes sense, if you think about it. They're so miserable with each other, of course they're fascinated by you.

When they weren't asking me questions about my Jewish father and gentile mother, they were busy cursing each other out. These two fought constantly, which I didn't have a problem with. It's so much better than watching a couple who can't get enough of each other and sit around making googly eyes back and forth. I had a roommate who had a boyfriend and all they did was make eyes at each other. He was all emotion all the time, constantly talking about his feelings and his profound love for her. He was minutes away from getting his first period. He wrote her poems too. It's my personal belief that if men are writing poems, they're making up for something else. Like a big hairy back, or one ball. Not that one ball is a bad thing. Especially since I don't know any females who are dying to get their hands on a set of balls. The way I see it, the less balls, the better.

Anyway, this couple wasn't the ogling type. If you put a napkin between these two they'd figure out a way to argue about it. So they bickered all day while I proceeded to get viciously burned in the sun. My mom had just sent me one of those traveling cases, where you put your shampoos and creams into little unmarked containers so you don't have to travel with big bottles that might spill. What I thought was sunblock turned out to be foot cream. I was wondering why the smell was so pungent. My mom spent my entire childhood taking naps while I was stranded at the mall or Hebrew school for hours at a time, and now all of a sudden I'm twenty, and she wants to pack my bags.

This wasn't the first time I'd looked like an asshole. This was, however, the first time complete strangers referred to me as "the asshole." I decided white would be a good contrast for my blistering tan at the party that night and a great way to get the attention I deserved.

The party was a blast. It was about a five-minute walk from our hotel at some millionaire's beachfront mansion. Everyone was salsa dancing around his pool as the waves crashed on shore. There were belly dancers on balconies. There were margarita-shaped ice sculptures that were made out of actual margaritas and people were slowly disrobing. Everyone was incredibly friendly, and I had a sneaking suspicion that some sort of Ecstasy was involved but I abstained because these weren't my people and, besides, I make it a personal rule never to experiment with drugs while having such a brutal sunburn. Alcohol, on the other hand, is never off-limits.

Then I saw him. My little midget, wearing a sombrero filled with chips and salsa on his head! It was the most adorable thing I had ever laid eyes on. As if my night could get any better, he was topless but wearing an apron and white pants. I thought I'd died and gone to heaven.

We hung out all night. I couldn't stop hugging him. He was one of the funniest midgets I'd ever met. Actually, he was the only midget I'd ever met—if you don't count the Internet. He had the cutest little hands and a high-pitched voice. He was shaped like a perfect sphere. He kept telling me one racist joke after another, and I couldn't get enough of him. At one point I had to send him away because I needed to catch my breath. My stomach was aching. He kept slapping my chest when he laughed, leaving what looked like puppy's pawprints all over me. Then he started barking. I love a guy who doesn't take himself too seriously. He was a tricky little Oompa Loompa too. He kept giving me shot after shot of tequila, and he kept getting taller, and taller, and taller.

His name was Eric and he was from Cleveland. I wanted to call him Nugget but thought I'd wait until after we became better acquainted. He had moved to Mexico to party for a year after he graduated from mortuary school. He figured his future was gonna be pretty grim, so he wanted to get in some hard-core fun first.

We talked and danced, and at one point I tried to pick him up, but he was heavy for a little guy. His mom was a midget too, but his dad was human-size. I guess his dad had a thing for little people, because he had married another midget before his mother. She had cheated on him with someone her own size, so he had gone on his way. I thought his father sounded like a great guy. So open-minded and such a broad thinker, to have fetishes for the little people too.

The sunburn combined with my fourteenth margarita was starting to cloud my head. I settled into a deep fog and didn't return to full 90 percent mental capacity until early the next morning.

The first thing I saw when I awoke were two tiny feet scurrying across the Spanish tile to the bathroom. I was so confused. At first I thought, Oh, great, I had a baby. Then I felt under the covers. My underwear was still on. I knew you could never have a baby with your underwear still on.

Then I heard what sounded like someone jumping off the toilet seat and landing on the floor. "Whew, these tiles are cold," said someone who sounded like he'd just inhaled an entire tank of helium. That squeaky little voice was too much. It all started coming back to me, and it was not good. My head was spinning and I was not in a good mood. I didn't know if things were going to get violent, but I did know one thing: Eric needed to be gone. But first I needed to know if I had slept with a midget, and I needed to know fast.

Then I saw it. His penis was the size of a boa constrictor. I couldn't believe it. My jaw dropped open and I stared for close to a minute in pure, titillated horror.

"Did we have sex?" I asked.

Eric was quick to blurt out, "We can if you want to."

My vagina immediately clammed up. I was scared for me and my little beaver's life. I just hoped we would make it out of this okay.

"You were really drunk last night," he said condescendingly. Wow, I guess nothing gets past this guy.

"Listen, Columbo, did we have sex or not?" I asked.

"Well, that depends on what you mean by sex," he replied. This guy was getting more irritating by the minute. All the cute stuff had worn off with the tequila, and I started to think of him like a piñata. Could I take this guy? Was I strong enough to fight a male midget?

Seeing I was angry, he hurried to answer. "No, I just pleasured you for a little bit, and then you passed out."

Thank God for alcohol. To think I might have actually had that thing inside my little girl scared Mommy.

Then I heard my sisters walk in the door.

My sisters are a very interesting duo. One of them is a converted Mormon. The other is sane.

Sloane, the Mormon, and I have had a very tumultuous relationship most of our lives. She seems to think I stole her thunder by being born. She was five years old and had claimed the throne of the youngest child with no thoughts of any competition. Her side of the story is that upon my arrival, she was thrust into a dark emotional corner, unable to express herself or get the attention she had gotten used to. Still reeling from middle-child syndrome, at the age of twenty my sister decided to distinguish herself from the rest of our family by converting to Mormonism. She believed this would be a way to carve out her own identity. Her plan was successful, although now her identity was the lunatic. We were slowly becoming closer in our twenties, but Sloane was very judgmental and something like bedding a midget could be a huge setback. Sidney, the older one, has always been my second mother. During my entire childhood, it was always Sidney who picked me up from Hebrew school when my parents forgot to and who asked for friends' phone numbers if I was going to stay at their houses overnight. My mom was way too relaxed as a parent. By the age of ten, if I told her I was going backpacking in the Himalayas for the weekend, she would have told me to have a great time and to definitely call her when I returned.

My whole family knows I have a propensity toward hedonism, but I don't think sleeping with a midget falls into that category. Or the category that falls under sharing the experience with anyone else in the world. Not for a while, anyway. I didn't want to see that look of disappointment on my sisters' faces for the next five days. I had to think fast.

I ran out into the living room and explained that I had a naked midget in my room because the hotel misunderstood me when I ordered room service.

They both looked at me with disgust on their faces.

Eric slipped out while my sisters waited in the other room. I, of course, proceeded to ream Sloane for renting a hotel room at a place that would provide that kind of service. "It's sick is what it is," I told her.

The following five days in Cabo did not go by without a jibe every time someone under five feet passed by, which in Mexico is pretty frequent.

"Chelsea," Sloane would say repeatedly as we sat poolside, "you've really hit an all-time low."

"Literally," Sidney would then chime in. Then the two would erupt into hysterical laughter, which was followed by snorts of disgust. It became clear to me on that trip that midgets are great for parties, but for me that's where it ends.

DESPERADO

HAVE YOU EVER experienced a pain so sharp in your heart that it's all you can do to take a breath? It's a pain you wouldn't wish on your worst enemy; you wouldn't want to pass it on to anyone else for fear he or she might not be able to bear it. It's the pain of being betrayed by the person with whom you've fallen in love. It's not as serious as death, but it feels a whole lot like it, and as I've come to learn, pain is pain any way you slice it.

I walked in on Peter, my boyfriend of two and a half years, with not one but *two* Asian women. It was similar to what I can only imagine a Hong Kong SWAT team must look like. They all seemed very happy, especially the one swinging from the ceiling fan. I can't say that there were any clues to my ex's propensity toward Asian women, but when you break up with someone and reflect on your time together, all the red flags you chose to ignore gradually become more and more obvious. For example, I used to think he just liked rough sex when he would pull my hair tightly in bed; I realized afterward that he was trying to get my eyes to go sideways.

Peter always had an inclination toward threesomes. He

had begged and begged me in his Cockney accent to seriously consider one. (His accent became annoying only after I found him in bed with the wok 'n' roll twins. Before then, it was impossibly charming.)

"Just try it, try it, you're really gonna like it. It's really popular in Europe," he would say over and over again. This could have been a compelling argument had the same not been true for David Hasselhoff.

After I discovered him in his threesome, I spent the next two weeks in bed suffering from a severe case of vagina elbow. It's a condition not unlike tennis elbow, but you get it from masturbating. My girlfriend Lydia called, for the twentieth time, trying to convince me to go out.

"I can't," I said. "I threw my back out masturbating."

"That's so disgusting," she said. "How the hell were you doing it?"

"Oh, please, Miss Goody Two-shoes. Like you've never gotten yourself from behind!"

It was clear to both of us I needed a night out and possibly a little nookie. Nothing reels you into tears like your first one-night stand after a breakup, and I just needed to get it out of the way.

Lydia was the kind of friend whom people referred to as a "party favor"—always fun to be around but she doesn't really have any patience for suffering unless it's her own. I have been friends with her for so many years that I overlook her shortcomings in the emotional department and focus on the positive. Any time you go out with her, for example, she is completely committed to having a good time. Besides, it was Lydia who went back to my English ex-boyfriend's after we broke up to pick up my things and key his car.

We went to our local watering hole on Tuesday night. It's called Renee's and it should be shut down by the Health Department. That is, if places could be shut down due to unsanitary customers. I was shamefully dressed. I had put on some old Gap capris and a men's white V-neck under-shirt with a pair of Adidas slides. I had no business being out in public. Not only did I look pathetic and unkempt, I had a severe case of camel toe that was starting to give me a headache.

There were only eight guys in the bar, so I found the one who most suited my needs. After three vodka Collinses I approached him.

He was definitely much older than me but could still be considered part of my generation. I want to say late thirties, but realistically it was more like early forties. The other options were unacceptable: two guys who didn't look a day over eighteen and another guy who had close to a dozen tattoos on one side of his face. I don't like to discriminate, but I prefer my men without any makeup. The only other man who wasn't sitting with a girl was whispering to him-self and laughing.

I was either going home with the older guy or going home with myself. I chose him. I could tell he was wrong right from the start. As I approached, he cocked his head back and gave me that silly look men give that says, "You like what you're looking at, don't you?"

I prefer the strong silent type. A little mystery, perhaps. I talk a lot and prefer it when men don't. This guy kept giggling like a schoolgirl and telling me how sexy I was. There are times when I actually am sexy, but this definitely was not one of them.

Lydia came over and looked at me like I was sitting next to a unicorn.

"What?" I asked her.

"He's disgusting," she said.

She was right. He was pretty disgusting. It wasn't that he was bad-looking, it was his personality—so wild-eyed and eager. It felt as if someone had just let him out of an asylum for the night, and he was getting his first taste of big-city life. He acted like I was Cindy Crawford and he had never had sex.

I didn't think I was going to be able to do this. I ordered a double. He smiled at me in a way I'm assuming he thought was debonair and said, "You know, you don't have to drink to make yourself more fun to be around." I wanted to tell him I was drinking so that *he* was more fun to be around.

When I finished my drink, I asked him if he wanted to get out of there and go back to his place. His euphoria was nauseating. He told me he was in a white Jeep Cherokee and I told him I'd follow him. I was driving a Toyota Echo at this point, which is a very silly car. It's so little you don't even have to put it in reverse; you just pick it up and turn it around.

Before we left, I informed him I needed to stop at 7-Eleven to get a sandwich. I hadn't really eaten anything of substance in two weeks, and the alcohol was bringing back my craving for something with cheese.

I ran into 7-Eleven while he waited in his car. I got a turkey sandwich out of their "deli case" and the largest bag of Doritos they sold. I hopped back in my car and proceeded to gnaw away at my Doritos and sandwich like a barnyard animal. It was like I was punishing this guy for being so willing. Did I really have to get Doritos, food that leaves your mouth smelling like a Dumpster? I'm surprised I didn't just get a block of jalapeño cheddar to suck on. It was like I was daring him to back out.

We got to his place, and it looked a lot like his personality. Just a bunch of space filler, nothing to really wow you. It looked like he had bought a lot of stuff from IKEA and then decided to refinish it at home. Everything was neat and tidy, but you wouldn't want any of it for yourself.

I sat down on his black pleather sofa and proceeded to make a spread for myself. He put on some Lou Rawls and went into the bathroom for a couple minutes too long. Maybe he was putting in his diaphragm. By this point I was really considering leaving, but I was enjoying my sandwich and chips too much. Also, I was trying to figure out who the bigger loser was, this guy, or me for being at his apartment.

A couple more minutes passed and then I heard someone whistling. I had to assume it was him because my mouth was full. Then the bathroom door swung open and he walked out.

Now, I've seen guys do some crazy things in the movies but never in real life. He was buck naked, except for a leather neck brace/helmet and a black leather holster. There was a set of shackles around his ankles, but they weren't connected, and he was holding a flashlight.

I had no idea what to make of this. After staring at him for thirty seconds with my mouth full, I managed to ask, "What's up with the flashlight?"

The smile on his face made me wonder if he might be a serial killer.

He started playing with his penis. It was time to put down the sandwich.

"I want you to hit me," he said with a big ugly grin.

I didn't want to appear frightened, so I played along. "I love hitting guys," I told him. I couldn't figure out if he was crazy or just plain stupid. I decided he didn't fit the profile of a serial killer—he was too outgoing.

I was not sleeping with this idiot. *No one* should have to sleep with this guy.

He came over to the couch and sat down on the side of me that was not occupied by food.

"I love kisses," he whispered, leaning in to make his move.

I held his chest back with my hand. I should have used my sandwich to block him. I was trying to remember if I had my camera in my car. Getting some pictures of him would be fun for years to come, but that would mean spending more time with him.

"Wait," I said, in my most seductive voice. "I have something in my car that I think you are really going to go nuts over."

He got excited. "What is it?" he asked.

"Oh, you're really going to like this."

"How do you know I don't already have it?" he cooed.

"Oh, believe me, you don't have this," I said.

"Okay, sexy, you go get it for Daddy."

This was getting good. I loved that he referred to himself as my father. My dad was going to really get a kick out of this one.

I collected all my belongings, including what was left of my sandwich and bag of Doritos. He asked me why I was taking my food, and I said it was part of the surprise.

Right before I got up from the sofa, I turned and smacked him in the face. I couldn't pass up the opportunity to hit this guy. His nostrils flared and his smile grew so big I thought his head might split open. I smacked him once more for good luck.

I sashayed up to the door without breaking eye contact, walked outside, and went to my car. Then I got in, started the engine, and turned around just in time to see him standing in his doorway, buck naked in his get-up, with his penis dangling in front of him.

I rolled down my window and waved good-bye. He started to wave back and then stopped and looked confused.

If I were a believer in the theory of "rock bottom," this could very well have been it. As it stands, I am not a believer. Rock bottom is for sissies; I've hit rock bottom dozens of times. I've woken up next to a billy goat, for Christ's sake. You don't just give up!

The result of going home with someone just for the sake of getting back at a boyfriend only ended in disappointment with myself. This clearly wasn't the guy for me or any other human. And sometimes going through the roller coaster of emotions instead of trying to distract yourself from it helps the pain move along more quickly. Even if times are tough and you're enduring a terrible heartache, it's important to focus your anger on a vibrator, not another person.

SKID MARK

I WAS AT a little bar in Brentwood called El Dorado with Lydia. One of the reasons I like Lydia so much is that she's easy. The minute a glass of cheap chardonnay hits her collagen-injected lips, she is minutes away from being on her back. We're a great team.

This is also a girl who once sat me down to tell me she had joined a club called Sex Addicts Anonymous, and in response to my laughing said, "Chelsea, it's very serious. It's about being addicted to having sex with strangers."

"Isn't that just being a whore?" I asked her.

She went to a few meetings and then quit, once she realized that any sort of promiscuity was not going to be cured by fifty other people who were all trying to have sex with her.

At El Dorado, we came upon two cute boys whom we had met a couple months before when Lydia went home with one of their friends. She and the guy never spoke again, a true one-nighter. Apparently, Lydia's dream of getting gang-banged by an entire football team never came to fruition, so she at least wanted to frequent the same circle of guys. Then, whoever was videotaping these affairs would be able to piece it together like a real live gang bang. See? Dreams can come true.

More important, their friend Gavin was a babe. Beautiful. The kind of face no one could say was eh. He was about five-ten and lean but muscular, with black hair and bright blue eyes. He was Ricky Martin cute minus the bounce in his step. He was a bit standoffish and I smelled a challenge.

Since I hadn't had sex with anyone they knew (not that they were aware of, at least), I was deemed the sweet, naive "good girl." I took on my new role with conviction. I talked of the all-girls private school I never attended, the Peace Corps in Guatemala that taught me so much, and how, if I played my cards right, one day I might head up the American Red Cross. It was a winning performance. At one point this guy asked me if I was Christian. I nodded piously and told him that while I don't agree with Jesus on absolutely everything (like not having sex on the first night), I did believe you had to live a life full of morals and goodwill.

I excused myself to do a little mingling, mostly because I had gas and didn't want to let one loose in front of Gavin, but also because I didn't want Gavin to take me for granted. Minutes later I returned and continued to conversation-rape him about my fictitious life full of noble dreams, hopes, and ambitions. I told him how the year I spent volunteering at the Boys & Girls Club of Santa Monica had really helped put me in touch with the urban youth. "Tomorrow's future" was the term I used. I could not stop lying, throwing out one ridiculous story after another. I was having a blast.

"What is that smell?" he asked as he crinkled his face in disgust.

My fart had ricocheted its way back to me.

"Ugh, gross, somebody totally farted. That is disgusting. People have no manners," I said to him, shaking my head.

Then I got a little cocky. I made my father Cuban with an indecipherable lisp who couldn't read or write. I confessed to Gavin how hard it was to grow up with a father who traveled to the States by way of an inner tube, and that all the kids used to call me Elián Gonzáles. This is when Gavin started to clue in, considering that Elián Gonzáles had gained notoriety only the week before, and I was talking about a time twenty to twenty-five years ago.

My gas was really acting up, so I decided to cut my losses, go to the bathroom, and take a dump. Boy, did I ever. I made a mental note to myself never to eat Mexican on weekends and came back to find Lydia making out with Gavin's friend.

She caught me by the back of my hair and whispered, or tried to, "We're going home with these guys."

I quickly pulled her aside and told her about my massive accomplishment in the restroom and that due to their lack of a bidet and toilet paper, I should probably go home and clean my butt. She reminded me that she had acted as my wingman on more than one occasion prior to this and that a good friend will help you sleep around. Why we both needed to have sex on the same night was beyond me, but I was interested in seeing Gavin without his shirt on, so it didn't take much to twist my arm. Gavin seemed like someone who would have soap at his place, so I took comfort in the fact that at some point, my ass would be addressed.

We got back to Gavin's place and I immediately ran to

the bathroom. I washed myself with soap but didn't feel right about wiping with one of his towels, so opted for toilet paper instead. Big mistake. I had used way too much water to clean myself and the toilet paper basically fell apart in my butt and got stuck there.

The real mistake turned out to be Gavin. He had a flat ass. One of the biggest turn-offs ever. I prefer a little something to hold on to. Guys can be on the skinny side, but a rear is a special thing to me. Gavin's ass wasn't just flat, though. He had a pancake in the place of an ass. A shovel, if you will.

What a disaster. The sex was okay, but for some reason I lost interest...or consciousness. Whichever. I awoke to a blinding sunlight burning into the room at around seven a.m. This guy didn't even have blinds on his windows. This place was turning into some sort of torture chamber.

I climbed over him to get myself dressed so I could skedaddle when there they were at the foot of the bed: my panties. Along with one giant skid mark straight down the center.

I immediately looked over to see if Gavin was awake, and when I saw he wasn't, I lunged toward the evidence. I grabbed my panties and did something I'm still not sure I understand. I threw them out his window into his backyard.

I scooped up the rest of my clothes and ran into the bathroom. As I got dressed, I tried to piece together the previous night's events, to get an idea if Gavin had seen my stain. I couldn't remember the exact moment my underwear came off. All I could recall were flashes of the two of us rolling around and, at one point, falling off the bed. I started going over different names I could adopt, other cities I could live in.

The door was cracked partway open and I heard footsteps coming toward me from the other bedroom. I peeked my head out.

Lydia was striding down the hallway into the bright, bright light, wearing nothing but black wool men's dress socks. Up to her knees. A series of thoughts ran through my head: Did Gavin and his friend live with their grandfather? Did Lydia have a threesome with their grandfather? Did she have an extra toe she was trying to hide?

There was dried mascara streaked down both sides of her cheeks and her hair was insane. She looked like a streetwalker. She explained the socks by saying she hadn't had a pedicure in two weeks and that her feet were starting to resemble something out of *Jurassic Park*. Then we heard a dog barking in the yard.

"Whose dog is that?" Lydia said.

Cujo's barking grew louder and louder. I heard a loud groan come from Gavin's room. That meant that contact was inevitable.

Lydia crept back to her bedroom, while I finished pulling on my outfit from the night before and raced to Lydia's door, screaming about my aunt's baby shower.

"Lydia! Lydia! I totally forgot! My aunt's shower is this morning. I'm late."

My aunt's tubes were tied about five years prior to that night, but I've always been good in a pinch. That is, until I saw Cujo running toward me with my panties in his mouth.

Gavin grabbed me from behind and started to nuzzle

my neck as I stood in frozen horror, watching the dog approach. I just kept hoping that at least the soiled part of the panty had been digested. Please, Jesus, please.

"Oh, shit, your underwear!" Gavin exclaimed. Here it was. I either had to come clean or completely turn the tables.

So I lied.

"Ah, I don't think so, asshole, I'm wearing mine." Before he could check, I mustered up some tears and ran back to the bedroom, plowing into some serious acting skills.

"Oh, I get it, Mr. Man," I sobbed. "You just bring girl after girl after girl after girl after girl back to your place whenever you feel like it, is that it? What, and then you collect their panties? Should I take mine off and leave them here for your collection too? Would you like that?"

I didn't want to lose momentum, so I didn't wait for his response.

"I confided in you! I was a virgin up until a month ago! And I thought we had a real connection. You really are some piece of work, mister!"

"Listen, I have no idea whose panties those are. I've never seen them before in my life. I honestly thought they were yours."

Then Cujo wandered into the room chewing on the remains of my panties. I thought I was home free. Then I saw a piece of the stained underwear hanging from his lower jaw.

The look of disgust on Gavin's face was mortifying. "Ew," was all I heard on my way out.

I got in the car and slammed the door. As I was pulling

away, I saw Lydia running out the front door in only her shirt and the grandpa socks. I was hoping she would have retained a little of my dignity, but apparently not. Clutching her jeans and shoes she screamed, "Wait for me!"

I slowed the car in order for her to jump in but refused to stop completely. She hit her head on the door as it was closing. "What is your fucking problem?" she said.

I told her the story, and soon the mascara stuck to her face was no longer dry. We were both hungry and decided anywhere public was out of the question. So we opted for McDonald's and as we pulled up, saw a sign that read, "The McRib is back."

"Back from *where*?" I asked.

"I dunno, but you better not have one," Lydia said.

It took me many sleepless nights to get over the humiliation of what had taken place. Where did I go wrong in life? I thought to myself over and over again. I would lie awake wondering how many pairs of underwear a Mexican goes through in a year. Once the initial mortification wore off, I realized that like many things in life, this was a gift. I wouldn't have to learn twice about avoiding Mexican food on the weekends. Who knows how many girls I've helped by sharing my story?

THUNDER

ONE OF MY girlfriends was getting married. This was becoming an annoying pattern. Sarah was my third girl-friend to get engaged within six months, and it was becoming clear to me that more and more people were going to go through with it. It's not the concept of marriage I have a problem with. I'd like to get married too. A couple times. It's the actual wedding that pisses me off.

The problem is that everyone who gets married seems to think that they are the first person in the entire universe to do it and that the year leading up to the event revolves entirely around them. You have to throw them showers, bachelorette weekends, buy a bridesmaid dress, and then buy a ticket to some godforsaken town wherever they decide to drag you. If you're really unlucky, they'll ask you to recite a poem at their wedding. That's just what I want to do—monitor my drinking until I'm done with my public service announcement. And what do we get out of it, you ask? A dry piece of chicken and a roll in the hay with their hillbilly cousin. I could get that at home, thanks.

Then they have the audacity to go shopping and *pick out their own gifts*. I want to know who the first person was who said this was okay. After spending all that money on a bachelorette weekend, a shower, and often a flight across the country, they expect you to go to Williams-Sonoma or Pottery Barn and do research? Then they send you a thank-you note applauding you for such a thoughtful gift. They're the one who picked it out! I always want to remind the person that absolutely no thought went into typing in a name and having a salad bowl come up.

I prefer giving cash. When I get married, I'm gonna register at Bank of America. Both times. I'm a Jew. I don't mess around when it comes to money.

But it doesn't end after the wedding. Next they want you to come over and watch the wedding video. Like I really want to see footage of me passed out in a cake.

A wedding can really put a damper on a good friendship. Once people get married, they think they've got the whole world figured out. Immediately they think all their single friends are sad and pathetic.

"Oh, why don't you come over Friday? We're gonna have a bunch of people over and play some board games. Maybe you'll meet someone nice." What a hoot. My response is always the standard, "Unless you're playing Who's Hiding the Ecstasy?, I don't think I'm gonna be able to make it. I've got plans." Don't married people know that the last thing a single person wants to do on a Friday night is play a nutty game of Yahtzee? I'd rather take a bubble bath with my father.

And then there was Sarah's bachelorette party. Las Vegas and I have a special relationship. We never let each other down. Olympic Gardens is touted as the best strip club in

Vegas, and for good reason. Eight of us went there on the very first night, and I will never forget the look on all of our faces when we saw our man. They announced his name, "THUNDER," and I thought, Excellent.

THUNDER was beautiful. This wasn't a *Playgirl* pinup type with long hair and a bowtie who could rival Fabio in a "Who's Grosser?" competition. This guy was Dylan McDermott good-looking, with an ass that could double as a shelf—by far the most beautiful body any of us had ever laid eyes on.

All the girls were drooling and signing up for personal dances with him onstage. It quickly became clear what had to be done. I had to take one for the team.

I had never seen all my girlfriends go goo-goo over the same guy. Most of them were in relationships and two were already married. Each one of us was in her own personal fantasy of what could be done with a body like that, and I knew I had to be the one to act on it. I saw Lydia and Ivory out of the corner of my eye start to drool and told them to step off. "He's mine."

Other than that I didn't have much competition, except for every other girl in the club. Well, they could have him too—I just wanted a piece of the action. One of my friends bought me a dance with him and I was called onstage. Now, I'm not a big fan of strip clubs to begin with. I like a little mystery, and it's my personal belief that men look better in clothes. I was wrong. I got my dance—and his ass in my face—but I managed to keep my cool. He had the most adorable face I had ever seen. Sweet baby blue eyes, dark hair, and the cutest smile to hit that side of the Vegas strip.

While he was dancing around me onstage, he asked where I lived and I told him L.A. He said he lived there too and just drove here on the weekends to work. A commuting stripper. Talk about dedication to your craft. I wrote down my number and bid him adieu. My work there was done.

The girls made me promise I'd go out with him.

"Go out with him? I'm not *going* anywhere with him. I will go to him and then I will have him."

Immediately I wondered how much weight I would need to lose to be acceptable to a stripper. All he saw were other girl strippers and their perfect bodies. Maybe I would just tone up. These thoughts took over my brain for the next few minutes until I found the limo and then the minibar.

THUNDER called me the next week. He tried to tell me his real name, but I quickly interrupted him. "I like THUNDER. Let's just stick with that for now."

"Okay, I guess, but no one really calls me that," his husky voice replied. This guy was giving me too many details.

"No matter," I said. "How was your drive back from Vegas?" I had to feign interest in all this nonsense until I could ask when I could come over and sit on his face. I didn't say that out loud, of course. I never say the things I really want to. If I did, I'd have no friends.

"Can I take you to dinner?" he asked.

"How about drinks?" I replied. I just wanted his address, but I didn't want to scare him.

We met at the Lava Lounge. I made sure it was somewhere close to his place. I told him I didn't want him driving too far after his drive back from Vegas.

He showed up in a flannel shirt and blue jeans. Nothing

too revealing, kind of like a lumberjack. Kind of like on a men's calendar. I stared at his flannel shirt, wondering whether it was material I could actually rip with my own two hands. I decided that it was going to be very rough sex.

As I downed a couple of vodka Collinses, I asked him questions about his life and what he planned on doing. "Well, I just turned thirty-seven" (that was a shocker, he didn't look a day over twenty-nine) "and now I want to start really focusing on my acting." Oh, my God. I looked around to see if anyone else had heard him.

"An actor?" I said, trying to sound intrigued. "Wow, that's so... You have a great look, I'm sure it won't be a problem."

Who in his right mind decides to get into acting at the tender age of thirty-seven? Weight lifting maybe, but acting? Was this guy serious? What had he been wasting his time with until then? Well, stripping, I guess. They say it's hard to walk away from that kind of money. THUNDER told me he made anywhere from three to four grand a weekend, which, compared to my $311 per week unemployment check, sounded like quite a handsome income. But forget taking this guy to Sarah's wedding. I'd never hear the end of it. I just smiled and thought, Keep on talkin', you hot piece of ass.

"So you're a comedian," he said. "Tell me something funny."

"Okay. The great thing about being an alcoholic is that when you're bored at a party, you can leave without saying good-bye, and people just think you blacked out."

"Are you an alcoholic?" he asked me.

"That's not really the point," I responded. "And I don't like the word 'alcoholic.' I like to think of myself as an advanced drinker."

"I'm confused," he said. It was pretty obvious that THUNDER spent a lot of his time being confused, so I switched the conversation back to his career.

There is only so much actor talk one person can take, and I had reached my limit. We needed to wrap this little chitchat up now. I excused myself to the bathroom, hoping that would give him some time to finish his beer, and we could move on to the action. In the restroom, I met two girls who were making fun of a guy one of them was talking to. Evidently, he had a pretty bad lisp. I told them that was nothing—if they really wanted to see funny, they should come and listen to THUNDER for a minute. "I'm not even sure this guy can read," I said and relayed the story of how we had met.

They got excited at the idea of meeting him, and the three of us all went back to the table together.

I made the introductions, explaining to THUNDER that I had run into some friends. They looked at each other and giggled. It was clear they were taken with his beauty. Who wasn't? Then one of the girls whispered to me, "Does he talk?"

I said, "Yes, he talks, he's not a chimp."

"Ask him a question," she persisted.

That's too mean, I thought. "What should I ask him?" I said with clenched teeth.

"Ask him how to spell something," she shot back.

That crossed the line. I started to feel bad about mistreating THUNDER. Flashbacks of being harassed in high school by older girls flooded my conscience. I had never wanted to be mean like that to someone, and now here I was acting just as bad. Possibly even worse, since I was technically an adult and should know better. And, at some point, he was going to catch on. He was a little slow, but he wasn't out-and-out brain-dead.

So we bid our adieus and jetted back to his pad. I told him I wanted to see his head shots.

Twenty minutes later I'm airborne and getting the bottom knocked out of me. This guy wasn't so stupid after all. He really knew his way around a woman. It was crazy, rough stuff. I couldn't get enough of him. He was flipping me around, pinning me this way and that. His skin was soft and he had a back you could just hold on to for dear life. His arms were solid muscle and he had this beautiful, perfect ass. Of course I had seen this all before when he was onstage, but now I was living out every girl and gay guy's fantasy. Soft lips too. Really good soft lips. I love men.

There's something truly wonderful about a man who knows how to take a woman. I thought maybe it was love. I even slept over. I knew I would be back for more. Who cares if he didn't know how to multiply? This guy was some sort of sign from God.

THUNDER and I started seeing each other on a regular basis. We got into the pattern of skipping the formalities of cocktails altogether, and I would just come over. The sex was amazing every time. I even enjoyed sleeping next to him. It felt like sleeping next to a rhinoceros. His body was so big, I felt petite next to him. I wanted to show him off to my friends, but I didn't want him to speak. I was torn.

I called him while he was driving back from Vegas one Sunday. He didn't seem happy to hear from me. I sensed something was wrong and that I would not be getting any action that night. He told me he was exhausted from driving and didn't know if he would be up for one of my visits. What? Too tired? I understood our Cirque du Soleil act required some stamina, but I felt it was well worth it. Then he laid it on me. He had met someone else whom he thought he wanted to get serious with.

"A girl?" I asked.

"Yes," he said. "You're a really great girl and we've been having a blast, but I think we both know that this is not something that's going any further. I just don't see myself getting serious with you."

Oh, my God. I couldn't believe I was getting dumped by THUNDER. I couldn't believe I was getting dumped by someone whose real name I didn't even know. My time in heaven was up, and I was being told I wasn't the marrying kind by someone who undresses for a living. Was it because I wasn't flexible enough? Not serious enough? We were seeing each other at least two times a week. How much more serious could we get?

"Are you there?" he asked.

"Yeah."

"I'm really sorry."

"It's okay. I understand," I lied. "So, is there any way I could still just see you tonight?" I asked.

Silence.

"Good-bye, Chelsea. I wish you well." He hung up. Well, onward and upward. It's not that I hadn't had my heart broken before, but this was the first time I heard my little beaver cry a little. Talk about sad. She didn't leave the house for days.

Shrinky Dink

A SMALL PENIS on a little boy is not a big deal. However, if that boy continues to grow and his penis does not, it turns into a very big deal. I feel terrible for men who have small penises. What are they supposed to do? I guess they could have penile enlargements, but are people really doing that? I hope so.

I had a brief summer fling with a small-penis person once. My only excuse is that he was a lot of fun to hang out with—and I was barely twenty. I didn't know at that point that it was okay to leave a guy in the lurch. I definitely *did* know that it wasn't okay to talk to him about his tiny penis. "By the way, will you let me know when you're inside me?" Plus, this guy was right after my black phase where I never came across a penis smaller than a baby's arm. I thought maybe it was the price I had to pay for going back to the white man.

Cut to five years later at a club called 217 in Santa Monica, and a little Ecstasy. 217 is a dance club, and in order for me to go to 217 and do what everyone else was doing, I had to take drugs. I like my Ecstasy in small quantities, and then I like it again in about an hour or so—in more small quantities. I don't like to overdose. Call me old-fashioned.

We were all in the mood for a wild night. Ivory had just broken up with her architect boyfriend from Holland. Ivory hadn't dated a guy without an accent since high school. Lydia was reeling from a terrible breakup with a man who'd treated her like shit for close to two years. I had seen him on plenty of occasions out at bars, where he would not only hit on her friends but then tell her about it. She thought he just needed to grow up. The guy was thirty-five, which in L.A. years is twenty-five, and it didn't look like he was going to get his act together now or later. The worst thing about him, though, was his terrible breath.

After their first date, Lydia had called me and said, "I really liked him, except he had smelly breath. So we went back to my place..."

"I'm sorry...?" I asked her.

"So we went back to my place..."

"Hold on a second. *After* you realized he had bad breath, you went back to your place?"

"Well..." She paused.

"Well, nothing!" I told her. "Listen, Lydia, halitosis is not the beginning of a relationship, it's the end of one. That's not something you can *work* through. Unless you have access to a tongue scraper that I don't know about."

Ivory and I had taken to calling him AB. Ass Breath. Long before the breakup, Lydia started using that nickname too.

Ivory, good old Lydia, and I were flying high on our three

tabs of Ecstasy. Thirty minutes after we got to the club, Lydia disappeared and Ivory and I were dancing. I saw a cutie watching me from the bar. My favorite are white, dark-haired men with decent footwear and he definitely fit the description. He was probably wondering who gave me the right to dance, but he seemed amused. So did the rest of the onlookers. I jumped down from the little dance stage with a scissor kick, onto the main floor, and made my way over toward him. Know that if I'm dancing on a platform, what little inhibitions I have, have completely left the building.

"You're cute," I slurred.

His name was Buck. It was easy to remember because it rhymed with what we were going to do later. He was a little more stocky than I usually like, but in a sexy way, and had a nice olive complexion. I remember he had this great riotous laugh. I love a man with a good laugh. We danced a little together, then went to the back bar to make out.

Public groping has got to be one of my least favorite things. I find it really offensive and just plain nasty. Unless I'm the one getting groped. Then I don't have as much of a problem with it.

We were going at it for about an hour, drinking, smoking, kissing. Slobbering might be a better description. At one point my girlfriends came over, took one look at us, and guffawed. As if they were above making out in public. This coming from Lydia, who a week earlier had woken up on her bathroom floor.

At around one a.m., I started to hit a plateau and knew I

had only a couple good hours left of uninhibitedness. I told Buck to drive me home, and then I'd follow him back to his house. He lived in Santa Monica too and insisted on just driving us straight to his house, offering to take me home in the morning. I had been down that road before, and if there's one mistake I never make, it's not having my own wheels. I do not, under any circumstances, carpool.

I made up some lie about having an early morning meeting—a meeting doing God knows what. Buck insisted that he would drive me home early. That was it. I had to resort to some tough love.

"Listen, unless I have my car, I'm not coming over, and I think we both know that will make you very sad." He agreed and drove me home so I could get my car. Out of the corner of my eye, as I climbed into the driver's seat, I caught him grinning. This poor Echo. It had been through so much. The good thing about the Echo was that due to its size, people always asked if it was electric. I always lied and said yes.

A half hour later, we got to his place and he pulled into an underground parking garage, waving me in behind him. No way did I want to park in his underground garage. I thought he was trying to trap me. This guy was good. I started to wonder if I had slept with him before.

"I don't want to park in there," I yelled.

"What is your problem?" he yelled back.

"Nothing, I just don't like parking in garages."

"Why not? What do you think is going to happen?"

I just stared blankly in his direction. At this point, if this guy carried Mace, I think he would've used it on me. I was turning into a nightmare. He looked exhausted.

"How will I get out of the garage in the morning?" I asked.

"Drive?" he responded wearily. "You don't need a key or anything. The gate will open."

I sat and stared at him, bewildered.

"There's a sensor," he explained, "when your car pulls up." Now he was talking to me like I was eleven. I found this attractive.

"Okay," I said. He must have thought I rode to school on a short bus.

We got up to his town house. It was really nice. There were at least three Warhols that I counted and lots of Nambé crystal. I like men who have their act together. I had seen one too many carpet-stained, bong-infested, toilet paper–less male habitats. He had beautiful dark hardwood floors and it smelled as if Mr. Clean had spent the night.

Everything else was pretty high-end too. He had a lot of electronics. There was a huge plasma-screen TV along with every possible appendage that can go along with it. A lot of stainless steel. I found out later in life that stainless steel is a good countertop for intercourse. Anything with grout can leave marks and/or tear the skin.

He put on Fleetwood Mac, which I love, and I decided to reward him with a little striptease. I pushed him toward the bedroom and then started stripping in the doorway. He liked my dancing. The only explanation for that was that he was on Ecstasy too.

When I was done, I walked over and climbed on top of

him in my underwear. I pulled his clothes off until he was only in his boxers. Then I put my hand down his pants.

The thought had never even crossed my mind that he might have a little dinky. "Little" is a generous word when you're describing something the size of a canned Vienna sausage. This thing was smaller than my big toe. It wasn't even like a penis, it was like an extra piece of skin. I was mortified. I had to get out of there.

I was not doing charity work here. I couldn't have sex with him just because I felt bad. I'd feel worse after. I flung myself off of him and yelled, "Oh, my God, Oh, my God!!!"

"What," he said. "What is it?"

"My car," I shouted. "I forgot why I had to leave it on the street."

"Why?" he asked.

"Because Ivory has to come pick it up. She's staying with me."

"What? What are you talking about?"

"Ivory, she doesn't have a car. She needs to pick it up. I totally forgot. That's why I needed to park it in the street."

"Ivory, the girl you just left at the club? How the hell is she gonna know where your car is?" he asked.

"It has a homing device on it."

Silence.

"A homing device?" he asked. "Like a pigeon?"

"Yes!" I replied. "Just like a pigeon, and she won't be able to detect it when it's underground. I'll be right back."

Before he could say anything, I collected my things and was gone. Out of there.

Just like he said, the garage gate opened as soon as Echo

and I pulled up. Me and my Echo were going home. I didn't need to learn the small-penis lesson twice. It was time for some Jack in the Box.

When I told Ivory the next morning about how small his penis was, she said, "Gosh, Chels, you didn't need to leave him there, he could have been good at other things."

"Like *what?*" I asked her. "What?"

DON'T BELIEVE A WORD I SAY

YOU KNOW YOU'VE slept around a lot when you walk into your bank and see someone you've had sex with on a life-size poster for "Small Business Loans."

I have this really bad habit of lying compulsively when I drink. The thing is, it's never about anything I need to lie about. Sure, sometimes it's necessary to lie to get out of going to someone's party; sometimes we lie to avoid hurting people's feelings. Lying about your father inventing voice mail is a whole different ball of wax.

I once dated a guy for a couple of hours. I met him at a bar called El Dorado and managed to whisk him away after last call. He was a cutie and I wanted him in a bad way. He was funny, smart, and interesting—and mentioned something about spending every weekend in Mexico at an orphanage he had started.

When we were leaving, he hesitated about coming back to my place. This guy was playing hard to get, and I liked it. Fortunately, that act didn't last long, and we were soon on our way back to my apartment, which was conveniently located around the corner.

The sex was above average, and I was thrilled because

I really liked this guy and knew it would only get better. Then the next morning he rolled over and asked, "So, does your dad actually own American Airlines?"

I looked at him, bewildered. It took me about thirty seconds to connect the dots. I turned over so that I wasn't facing him and cringed. I would never be able to see this guy again. Great, I thought. Another guy I'll never get to know.

"Yeah," I said hesitantly. "Why? Do you want to go somewhere?" It would be easier never to return his phone calls than to fess up to being completely certifiable. I had to end it right there and, in turn, teach myself a valuable lesson: No lying while drinking. A normal person would have decided to stop lying completely. I decided to restrict myself to lying only when I was sober.

Cut to a couple of months later when I met this guy whose name I can't remember for the life of me. Let's call him Mike. There were a bunch of Mikes, so he was probably one of them.

I had a lot of free time because Ivory and Lydia were both dating guys and spending every minute with them. Normally I wouldn't have had a problem with this, but a month earlier, for my twenty-fifth birthday, the two of them had told every person invited to get me a vibrator. Ivory and Lydia were acting like they had never been through a dry spell before. True, it had been a good four months since a real relationship or any sex, but I was trying not to focus on the time frame.

Getting one vibrator at your birthday party is kind of funny; getting twelve is not. First of all, everyone completely ignored the fact that I was registered at Tom's Liquor's.

Second, how many vibrators does a girl really need? All it takes is one. What I am going to do, double-team *myself*?

I was working at a little breakfast place in Pacific Palisades at the time. Sometimes after work I would go to the Starbucks around the corner and read. I ran into him a couple times with his friend, and we did some heavy flirting. I was dying for it to lead to some heavy petting, but I was careful not to act desperate. This guy was right up my alley. He had dark hair and an adorable face and was very well built.

He looked like a cross between Tom Cruise and the Hulk. He was doing construction part-time at someone's house while trying to make it as an actor. The acting thing bugged me but wasn't a deal breaker. To compensate, I conjured up images of him one day owning his own construction company, bossing people around in a hard hat. While clearly this wasn't going to be a serious relationship, I definitely wanted him to take advantage of me.

On our third meeting, he finally asked if I wanted to "grab some chow." That's construction lingo for dinner. I remember blushing uncontrollably, which does not go with my personality at all. He kept telling me I was blushing, which made me blush even more. Guys love when you blush. I've tried to blush on cue but can never do it when pressured.

We went for sushi somewhere in Los Feliz. He was staying with a friend of his who was out of town, he told me. She was letting him crash until he found a place.

We had a couple of hot sakes and split two large Sapporos. I picked up the tab because I felt bad for him being a struggling actor. I don't know what I was thinking since I was working under the table at a restaurant three mornings a week to supplement my $311 weekly unemployment check. In addition to my addiction to alcohol, it seems I suffer from delusions of grandeur.

I invited myself back to his place. He accepted. I followed behind his gold Ford Pinto in my Toyota Echo. Talk about two losers.

We kibitzed while looking at his friend's artwork and pictures. They must have been really close because his family pictures were all over the place. He said she had been gone awhile shooting a movie, so he kind of made the place his own. It never occurred to me to be suspicious, probably because I wasn't auditioning him for a recurring role in my vagina. I knew I might see him again, but we were *not* going to become an item. It also never occurred to me that anyone lied as much as I did. If I had been interested in anything more than penetration, the Pinto would have sent me reeling back to reality.

I left soon after the sex because the bed was uncomfortable and I prefer to do my walks of shame in the evening, when it's not so bright.

We went out again a couple more times and got along pretty well. I even ended up sleeping over once—because I had one gin and juice too many. You may have noticed by now that I enjoy a plethora of different libations. I'm an egalitarian that way. I don't play favorites.

Our last night together, Mike and I went bowling, and I had one of my accidents. I picked a ball that was too small for my fingers and upon trying to release the ball into the lane—for what I fantasized to be a strike—the ball stayed on my hand and took me down with it. I did a complete somersault, rolling across the slippery wooden lane, ending up in the gutter. Every employee was at my service within seconds, for fear of a lawsuit. Mike and I laughed about it, but I could tell there was a part of him that was scared for me.

After that night together, things started to get a little awkward between us. I felt like I was growing to like him, that we were starting to feel like a couple. I left and didn't speak to him for a couple of days. I wanted to call him but resisted the urge. I didn't want to fall in love with a construction person/actor/Pinto driver.

I finally gave in and called him a week later. He got off the phone quickly and didn't call me back until the next day. Forget it, I thought. I wasn't interested in tracking someone down. I'd seen my friends survive relationships like that, and it looked so unappealing and time-consuming. That was quality time they could have spent drinking.

I had never mentioned to Mike that I worked part-time as a waitress, so you can imagine my surprise when, a few days later, I saw him walk into my restaurant with a gorgeous brunette who could easily guarantee my elimination in a swimsuit contest. Shit.

It was eleven thirty in the morning and I was the last waitress left before the lunch girls came in. I could not believe Mike was sitting at a table that I was going to have to wait on. The only other option was to walk out, drive home, and never speak to another person from that restaurant again. Unless I could devise some scheme that involved a relative dying.

My mind raced as I considered my options. Even if a relative *had* died, there was no reason I couldn't physically wait on a table until someone showed up to relieve me. It was all too complicated. Also, the owner of the place had done me a huge favor by paying me under the table, so I couldn't possibly bail on her. I thought maybe I could have the busboy wait on Mike, or maybe the cook, but they all laughed at me when I asked. I didn't know if they were laughing because it was the first time they had seen me in a frenzy, or because they didn't speak English and thought I was telling a joke.

I had to think of something. Going over and introducing myself was not an option. I had to find another way.

Then I got an idea. It was simple. I would not be me. He didn't know that I worked here. I would just be someone who looked a lot like me. I would be my own twin sister. Yes! I could do this. I could pull this off. Why not? He didn't know anything about me. I *could* have a twin sister.

I walked over with a bounce in my step.

"Hi, guys," I said sweetly. "Can I get you a couple of drinks?"

The color immediately ran out of his face. Probably into mine.

"Hi," he said with terrified recognition. I kept repeating the same thought in my head. I do not know this guy. I do not. I have never seen him before in my life.

"Hi," I answered. "Can I get you any drinks?"

Silence. He was just staring at me. And now *she* was staring at me too.

I will not give up on my plan, I thought.

"Drinks?" I asked again. Come on, nut bag, play along! I was helping him out of an uncomfortable situation too.

"Um, yeah. I'll take a coffee and, honey, what would you like?" he asked his little muffinhead.

"I'll take a coffee too please," she replied.

"Okeydoke, I'll be right back," I said with the gayest smile ever. I had become a cute, bubbly waitress with a positive disposition. I had just used the word "okeydoke" in a sentence.

The rest of the meal went pretty much the same way—me acting insane but all the time reacting to Mike as if *he* were the insane one. Every time he looked at me, I just looked back at him with big, crazy eyes as if wondering why this weirdo kept staring at me. Judging by the pallid, green color of his face, he was starting to feel sick. It was nice taking on the role of a friendly do-gooder waitress. I had never been so pleasant to customers before. It almost felt gratifying. I would have to look into that more later.

And so it continued. When the bill finally came, Mike ended up leaving me a 25 percent tip. I wondered if that was a result of his guilt or because of my sunny disposition. He left with his girlfriend, who smiled and waved goodbye. She was nice. I felt bad that she was dating someone who was a complete liar.

About twenty minutes later I was counting my money, getting ready to close out, and thinking about the irony of having paid for this guy's dinner a couple weeks earlier. What an idiot I was. Then, suddenly, I heard his voice.

"Chelsea." Oh, shit. It was Mike. Alone. I spun around to answer before it hit me that I was no longer Chelsea.

Panicking, I squinted my eyes to intimate confusion. "Are you speaking to me?" I said.

"I'm really sorry," he said.

"About what?" I asked, acting puzzled.

"About what just happened," he said. "I mean, yes, we're living together, but it's not—"

This is where it gets good.

"Okay," I said. "I need to stop you. I am not Chelsea. I know you've been looking at me very funny, but I'm not her. She's my twin sister. I don't know how you know her or what, but I have no idea who you are." Then I said ever so sweetly, "I'm really sorry."

Silence.

He stared for a bit. "Okay, this is really strange," he said. "You look exactly like her. I mean, exactly."

"Well, we're twins. That can happen with twins."

"So, what is your name?" he asked.

I hadn't prepared for that. What shall I name myself? I thought. All the names of people I'd been involved with started flooding my head. Unfortunately, none of them were girls.

"Kelsea," I blurted out.

"Chelsea and Kelsea?" he asked.

"You should meet our parents." I laughed. I quickly wondered if Chelsea had ever told him about our real parents. Then I reminded myself that I *was* Chelsea.

"This is unbelievable, you guys are identical!"

I nodded.

"But seriously, you look exactly alike."

Now he was getting on my nerves. Hadn't he ever seen twins before?

"Wait, why didn't she ever tell me she had a twin sister?" he said.

"I don't know, how do you know her?"

"We kind of um...well, we..."

I interjected. "Let me guess, you slept with her?"

"Oh." He felt stupid.

"Yeah, well, Chelsea pretty much sleeps with everyone."

"What?" He was appalled.

"Yeah, she's a real hoo-ha. This happens to me all the time. Men think I'm her."

"Does she do this all the time?"

I sighed. Hadn't I just said that? "Pretty much."

"You mean, she just sleeps with different guys all the time?"

"Afraid so. You should probably get tested."

Silence.

About five seconds passed before Mike sprinted out the door. He didn't even say good-bye, which I thought a bit rude.

"Should I tell her you stopped by?" I yelled after him.

"No."

He was gone.

About two years later I walked into my branch of Bank of America and saw his face plastered on their latest billboard for small business loans. It took me about ten good minutes to figure out how I knew this guy. I wondered if Bank of America would give me a small personal loan for having slept with their poster boy. I wondered if they would give me a small personal loan for sleeping with one of their tellers. I really needed a loan.

THE COOKIE MONSTER

I USED TO live with a twenty-eight-year-old virgin. That's right. Not a Mormon, not a religious thing, just plain stupid. You would've thought someone had sewn her vagina shut. Who in her right mind would willingly abstain from something that could give so much pleasure and pain at the same time? I asked myself again and again. I just wasn't getting it. And neither was she.

Dumb Dumb and I were like the odd couple. Dumb Dumb was tall with tight curly red hair and looked like a full-grown Annie. I would sashay around the living room in my brand-new thong and bra combo, while she'd lie on the sofa in a pair of her favorite Winnie-the-Pooh jammies buttoned to the top, slurping down a pint of Ben & Jerry's. She would bake cookies, watch nothing but reality TV, and talk on the phone for hours with her parents in New Jersey. I would come home sloshed three or four nights a week and the others I wouldn't come home at all. Since I was also two years her junior, Dumb Dumb took this to mean that she was in charge. If we ever went anywhere together, she would drive, and every apartment bill was put in her name so she could oversee all payments. She also had a severe case of OCD, so after I went to bed she would come out of her room, make sure all the appliances were turned off, and rewash any dishes I had washed. You would have thought I was living with Rain Man.

I'm convinced that Dumb Dumb's parents were the reason for her social ineptitude. She relied on her father for guidance on everything from what deodorant to use to what brands of electronics to buy. Not only did she not have any sexual contact in the two years we lived together, she rarely went out at night. She preferred to stay in and watch *The Bachelor* on the seventy-two-inch television her father bought her for our two-bedroom apartment. The resolution was so intense you couldn't even make out what was on the screen while sitting on the sofa in front of it. We'd have to stand in the dining room close to the front door to get a clear image. More important, she didn't like alcohol. There are two kinds of people I don't trust: people who don't drink and people who collect stickers.

I always dreamed of Dumb Dumb going on *Howard Stern* and playing Stripper Jeopardy. She thought the Senate was a type of cookie. I asked her once during an election if she could name the two presidential candidates. She said, "Duh, Gore and Bush."

I said, "Okay, and who's Gore's vice president?"

She said, "I'm not that stupid...Bush."

Her room was covered in roses and 'N Sync posters. You would've thought she hadn't gotten her period yet. She took a bath every night and never took showers. She cried the first time she was pulled over by a cop. I explained to her that there is no reason to cry when getting pulled over—unless you're coming directly from a crime scene.

We were living together on 9/11 and she was convinced it wasn't a big deal because her father had told her everything would be all right.

"My dad said it's gonna be okay, and they may have already caught the guys who did it."

It was as if the whole event had been an episode of *Charlie's Angels*.

About a week later I was driving her to the dealership where she had just bought a new car. The country had been on many different levels of "high alert" and no one knew when we would be invading Afghanistan. I was saying how it was so scary to know that at any minute we could go to war.

She panicked and said, "Oh, my God, is that today?"

Dumb Dumb worked at a flower shop, which was the perfect job for her. She supported her insanity by placing herself in an environment where everything really *was* coming up roses. It was the ideal environment, allowing her to be completely and happily oblivious of the world around her. Every Monday through Friday she would wake up at the crack of dawn to sell flowers. I never quite understood why people needed to get flowers at seven a.m. on a Tuesday and found it curious that somebody could get excited by anything other than a pancake that early in the morning.

Dumb Dumb had a major crush on some reality television show host who used to eat breakfast next door to the flower shop every morning. She spent most of her time standing in front of the flower shop in order to see when he sat down at the café. Then she would act surprised when he appeared and go over to say a "casual" hello. There are many forms of stalking and, combined with driving by his house several nights a week, this was one of them. I urged her to stop wasting expensive petroleum on trips to his house and instead put that effort into breaking his cell phone code and checking his messages.

Every afternoon she would come home and go on and on about this guy. How today he told her she looked pretty and smiled before ordering his eggs. She would ask me if I thought it was a sign that they both loved hard-boiled eggs. "Only if you're on an Easter egg hunt," I told her. Then she would get on the phone with her parents and replay every minute of their conversation. What a disaster. If I ever called up my father talking about a guy, he'd pretend he wasn't getting any reception. On a landline.

Despite the fact that all they'd done was talk about eggs and their deep respect for the Easter bunny, Dumb Dumb was convinced that this guy was going to come bursting out of her television screen and propose to her. She had the emotional maturity of a seven-year-old. Put us together, and we were fifteen.

Her crush had been raging for close to a year, and finally I couldn't bear it anymore. If she wasn't gonna stop talking about it, I was going to help her get him. First, though, she needed to get penetrated.

It was time to hire a male prostitute. I had used him once before, to "rough up" my friend Lily right after a breakup. She was pleased with him, a little too pleased. She got attached to him, and he had to start pseudo dating her, which cost me a fortune. He finally had to let her down easy because my unemployment ran out. But at least she had gotten over her ex.

Ed was great. Hot face, hot body. He was sweet natured, which kind of got on my nerves, but I knew Dumb Dumb would love it. And while I wouldn't call him stupid, he definitely wasn't home separating ions in his spare time. I had met him at a bachelorette party, thrilled to encounter my first male hooker. I had strolled the Hollywood strip many a weekend night looking for a soul mate but never found anyone who actually resembled a man.

Ed felt bad after what happened with Lily, so when I called him about Dumb Dumb, he told me he'd throw in a little extra. I didn't quite know what that implied but hoped it meant anal.

To set up the rendezvous, I took Dumb Dumb to a Backstreet Boys concert—the only way that I could get her out of the house. There have been a couple of times in my life where I have considered killing myself, and this was one of them. Watching these five guys prance around onstage made me question so many things about our culture. One, where were their instruments? Two, were there actually women out there who were turned on by this? Unfortunately, I was chaperoning one who was. Dumb Dumb was just about climaxing. Not like she would have known what had happened if she had.

I had Ed meet us there and we would "accidentally" bump into him. Then he would introduce himself as the Backstreet Boys' manager and allude to the idea of going backstage. He looked really good that night, and Dumb Dumb actually spotted him before I did, pointing him out as the cutie standing by the bar.

"Oh, my God, I know that guy! That's Ed. I've met him a bunch of times!" I said. "What on earth is he doing here?"

The look of excitement on her face was enough for me to call it a night. This plan was going to work.

We went over to him, and I made the introductions. "Dumb Dumb, this is Ed. Ed, this is my roommate, Dumb Dumb."

Ed gave her his newly bleached smile and said, "Well, Dumb Dumb, Chelsea never told me she had a roommate who was cuter than her." This guy was good.

"Really? Oh, my God, you're soooo funny."

This was her standard response to anyone she liked, whether what he said was funny or not.

I left them alone to scope out my own man, but within a few minutes I started to feel sick. My stomach was churning and I had broken into a cold sweat. As I leaned against the wall for balance, doubled over from nausea, it hit me. The Backstreet Boys were actually making me ill. I really had to get out of there. Luckily, this could work in favor of my plan. I couldn't believe I hadn't thought of it on my own.

I went back inside to find Dumb Dumb and Ed and explain that I wasn't feeling well. Just as I had suspected, they were sitting together in a booth, where he was regaling her with stories of God knows what, and she was eating it up. I asked Ed if he would mind driving Dumb Dumb home because I wasn't feeling so hot.

She looked a little scared for a second, but he assured her

that she would be in good hands and he would be nothing but a gentleman. I gave Ed a look to make sure he didn't mean that.

The minute I stepped outside and could no longer hear the music, I felt much better. My girlfriend Jen was going to some male model party that night so I decided to give her a call. She didn't even answer her cell phone with "hello"; she just picked up and said, "Get your ass over here now if you know anything about anything." Jen was Ivory's roommate, and I had grown to like her just as much—mostly because, unlike Ivory, she could hold her liquor and didn't believe in long-term relationships. Jen was the kind of girl who went out only once every so often, so when she did, she meant business. This was gonna be good.

I got to Falcon at a little after eleven. Plenty of time to make some one-night connections. There were models everywhere. The unfortunate thing was that there were some female ones too. Good. A challenge.

I found Jen surrounded by three guys who were all named Ross. She threw one my way, and Ross and I grabbed a table in the back.

Over drinks, I told him all about my roommate and the night's secret mission, and he thought it was hilarious. He must have laughed at everything I said, which can be very annoying, but only in the morning.

Ross told me how much he hated modeling, and all the pressure, and blah blah blah. His teeth were so white I found myself wondering what kind of teeth-bleaching agents models had available to them that weren't available on the regular marketplace. He was a little predictable, but I'd met a lot worse.

I thought he had potential in the game of life if he played his cards right. He definitely had potential in the game of my vagina, but who didn't?

All the other Rosses joined us, along with Jen and some model girl she befriended. Jen befriends everyone. In this case, I had no objections, because the minute this girl opened her mouth, Dumb Dumb seemed like a nuclear physicist. Here was proof that lots of people are indeed very challenged. She kept giggling and talking about her parrot who couldn't stop saying "poop." Like "poop" is such a naughty fucking word. Eventually, everyone started ignoring her, and I think she may have finally fallen asleep at the table.

Jen and I had some alone time while Ross 1, 2, and 3 went to get some more cocktails. A minute later, I noticed Ross chatting up some other girl at the bar. I'm not the jealous type, but I had to lay down the law.

"Hey, Ross!!" I shouted. Three guys turned to look in my direction. "No, you." Not wanting to be rude, I pointed at my Ross with two fingers instead of one. "Who are you talking to?"

He smiled and said, "I'm sorry, I'll be right back."

"No, no, it's okay," I said. "You can talk to other girls, but when I leave, you're coming with me."

He smiled again and said, "Yes, okay."

Perfect. I had landed my man and now I could hang out with Jen. I didn't really have much more to say to Ross anyway, and I'd better save what little I did have for later just in case I found myself in a pinch. Jen went on to tell me how Ivory's current boyfriend, Wang, likes to clip his toenails in their living room as well as make fruit smoothies every morning, and then leave the dirty blender in the sink.

"That's annoying," I told her. "Dumb Dumb would never stand for that."

"And how is Strawberry Shortcake?" asked Jen.

"Well, judging by the way I left things, she should be really good."

I told her about Ed, and after staring at me for close to thirty seconds with her mouth open, she said. "Wow, you're a *really* good friend."

"Well, I can't help it if I'm a giver," I told her. Last call came around and I collected my man. He followed me back to my place in Santa Monica and parked in the street, and then we tiptoed inside.

Quietly, we sneaked across the apartment toward my room. Dumb Dumb's door was shut so I assumed that Ed was in there popping her cherry. I don't know if I slipped myself a roofie or what, but the next thing I can remember is hearing Dumb Dumb screaming at the top of her lungs and Ross nowhere to be found.

I looked at my clock. It was four thirty a.m. I threw on a T-shirt and ran into the hall to find Ross standing there naked and Dumb Dumb in a pair of *Finding Nemo* pajamas still screaming. Apparently Ross thought the toilet was in her room and was so disoriented that he went in there and started peeing. On her.

I had never taken a guy home to my apartment before

because I knew Dumb Dumb had an aversion to strangers, especially men. I thought it would be okay that night because I figured Ed would be there too. Then in the morning, the four of us could fill each other in on the details of the previous night, and Dumb Dumb could make us all heart-shaped pancakes.

Boy was I wrong.

I couldn't even understand what Dumb Dumb was saying because it was at such a high pitch. The only other time I had seen her this upset was when I cut off her subscription to *Tiger Beat*.

I told Ross to get lost. It was clearly his cue to leave. He kept apologizing and apologizing, but it didn't help. He just looked ridiculous standing there naked.

I had to calm Dumb Dumb down. Of course, her first interaction with a penis had to be really up close with urine coming out of it. Not a dream come true. It took me a couple months after my first time having sex to even look at a penis. They're just so silly.

Innocently, I asked her where Ed was, and she said she had the best night of her life, but he didn't even kiss her good night. That bastard! If only Ed had been there, he could've knocked Ross out, and no one would be the wiser. Plus, I'd have had my bed all to myself.

I apologized profusely and told her how sorry I was about Ross. I assured her I'd get rid of him. Then I helped her change her sheets and wash the pee out of her curly red hair. But I knew, from that moment on, our relationship would never be the same.

When she finally calmed down enough so that she could

sleep, I went back to my room. Ross was passed out on the bed. He must have really felt terrible about pissing on my roommate's face.

"Ross. Ross. Rossss!" I yelled, slapping his face.

"That's not even my fucking name," he groaned.

"What?"

"That's not even my name." Now *he* was mad. Puhlease.

"You told me that was your name."

"No, you said that was gonna be my name because my other two friends were named Ross. You thought it would be funny if you called me Ross too."

"Whatever," I said. "Listen, there's street cleaning at six. You need to move your car."

"On a Saturday?"

"Yes," I said, "unfortunately." Then he asked if he could come back in afterward. Why, so you can urinate on me this time? I thought. "Sorry, I have to go to church very early," I said.

"But it's Saturday," he reminded me—*again*.

"Temple," I said. I think he got the message. If not, he definitely got the message when he realized our street didn't have any street cleaning. I decided that potty training, which had fallen off my list of prerequisites years earlier, would have to make a comeback.

It turns out that even Ed found Dumb Dumb too stupid. He apologized profusely but couldn't bear to break her heart and also couldn't bear to listen to her for another second. He told me there was only so much he could hear about *The Lion King*.

The next day I went out and bought Dumb Dumb a

karaoke machine and told her it would be a great way to jump-start her singing career.

"Really?" she asked. "Has anyone ever done that?"

"Uh, duh!" I told her. "How do you think Yanni got started?"

Ed felt pretty bad about the whole thing. He had never not fulfilled his job requirements before. So we both agreed it would be best if we slept together. Talk about fulfilling a requirement.

DOCTOR, DOCTOR

MOST WOMEN I know prefer female gynecologists, masseuses, and therapists. I prefer men. I've always felt that men have a better grasp of the female body, and I've always felt more comfortable naked with a man in the room. Their hands are usually stronger, they're usually more confident when performing the task at hand, and most men have penises. I love penises.

Ivory had just been referred to a new gynecologist. Apparently her last gynecologist started to give her attitude after seeing her three times in one month. She thought that maybe Ivory was a vaginal hypochondriac.

She was right. After any sexual contact or her period, Ivory would schedule an appointment with her OB-GYN to make sure everything was still intact. She tried to assure me these visits were driven purely by her desire to maintain maximum sexual enjoyment at all times. Knowing Ivory as well as I did, I was aware of the real reason: terror. She was constantly afraid of picking up a disease. This is someone who worried that her clitoris could catch unwanted UV rays from a maxipad that had been sitting in the sun too long. As if maxipads just decided to get up in the middle of the day and walk outside for a tan. She once asked me if I thought you could get crabs from giving someone a blow job. Knowing that crabs are attracted to hairy areas, I told her, "Yes, but only if you have a mustache."

After her first visit with Dr. Luke, Ivory came directly over to my apartment. She was beaming.

"You are never going to believe how sexy my new doctor is," she said. Ivory has excellent taste in men. I knew if she thought someone was sexy, he was. "He's funny, sexy, smart, and he's not married!" she cried.

"Great," I said. "Go out with him."

"I can't," she said. "I've been seeing Jackson for two months. We've decided to become exclusive."

Jackson and Ivory. Jackson was the lead singer of some band I can't remember the name of. He was pretty sexy, but his hair was longer than Ivory's and it always looked like he was hiding something in it. Ivory came from a lot of money; her Cuban parents had started a lucrative pet-grooming business that now occupied fourteen different locations. She usually dated rich men. She also wasn't one of those girls who went crazy for musicians, so I was surprised at their pairing. Other than seeing his band perform twice, I didn't know much about Jackson other than the fact that he loved going down on Ivory.

"Well, too bad," I said. "You'll have to wait until you break up, then. I'm sure you'll get to know Dr. Luke in the meantime."

"You go out with him," she said.

The thought of going steady with someone who knew his way around a vagina seemed like a great idea. "Okay," I said. "But first, I'm making an appointment. I have to make sure he's good with a speculum."

"You're the best! I knew you'd do it. You have to sleep with him too, though. I need to live vicariously through you."

"Well, let me see what I can do."

Ivory had never asked me for a favor before. I had done small favors for her, of course, bringing her medicine when she was sick or driving her to the airport, but nothing of this magnitude. I was honored that she trusted me enough to take on this task. She was in need, and luckily she had someone like me to depend on.

I called that afternoon to make my appointment with Dr. Luke. His first availability was in two weeks. Due to my lack of employment, my schedule was wide open and nothing conflicted on my end. And I couldn't think of a better way to spend my afternoon.

I immediately scheduled a bikini wax with my aesthetician. When I got there I asked her if she could wax a special message for the doctor. Like, "What's up, Doc?" She said my vagina face wasn't big enough for so many words. I loved the term "vagina face" and couldn't wait to use it in a sentence.

We agreed on the basic Brazilian—right after I downed a Vicodin. I don't know who thought up waxing, but it was clearly the same person who invented Vicodin.

Finally, the Tuesday of my appointment rolled around. I decided on a business suit to give the illusion of being a professional. The thought that I would be lying there naked escaped me.

When I got to the office, I was nervous. What if he didn't

like my vagina? What if I had some weird vagina that made him laugh? I usually wasn't this insecure, but I needed him to like me. I could not let Ivory down. Having someone depend on me really made me want to pull through. I filled out some paperwork and took a couple deep breaths.

When my name was called I went into the examining room and was given one of those cloth robes that doesn't close and has a bottom the size of a napkin, so if I was to sit up, my ass crack would be facing the door when Dr. Luke came in. This was not the first impression I wanted to make. I drew the robe shut and lay down.

Dr. Luke walked in. He was older, in his late thirties, and Ivory was right—very sexy. He reminded me of a friendly Richard Gere. Really warm. He flashed me a wide, genuine smile revealing a good bedside manner. I hoped this led to a good bedroom manner.

I liked him instantly. Ivory should be a matchmaker. I had my legs crossed and I was leaning up on my elbows. I looked like I was posing for *Playboy*.

"You are Miss…"

"You can call me Chesty—I mean Chelsea." I gave him my best smile. You would have thought we were at a picnic.

"Okay, Chelsea, you can call me Dr. Luke."

"Oh, thank you!" We both laughed. He was funny.

"And what seems to be the problem today?" he asked

"Oh, nothing in particular, just my annual Pap smear."

"It says on your chart here that your last Pap smear was two months ago."

"Really?" I asked. "That's weird, I could have sworn it's been a while."

"Well, your last doctor sent the test results over, and that's the date of the exam."

"He's actually not all there...*mentally,* if you catch my drift. That's why I'm here. I think his time as a doctor may be up."

"Oh, I see," said Dr. Luke. This was going badly. What was with the third degree?

"Well, let's get started," he said. "Why don't you lie back and relax. We'll just take a look and see if everything's in order."

I noticed pictures of him on sailboats all over his walls. "Are you a sailor?" I asked as he stuck something cold into my vagina.

"Yes, about every free chance I get."

"How weird," I said. "Me too!" If I had seen pictures of people eating each other on the wall, I would've told him I was into cannibalism.

"Really?" he asked. "How often do you go out?"

"Every chance I get."

"Do you have your own boat?"

"Yes. It's being fixed, actually, just a little Boston whaler." It occurred to me that a Boston whaler was not a sailboat. He asked what was wrong with it, and I panicked and said a flat.

"I mean...uh, not a flat, an oil leak," I said.

"Do you compete?" he asked me, as he peered up from in between my legs.

"Not really, but I love to watch. Sailing has always been my favorite thing to do."

I didn't even know what I was talking about. I wasn't

sure if I was making any sense at all, and I needed to steer the conversation elsewhere, before he found out that the closest I'd ever come to sailing was going down the water slide at Great Adventure.

"There's a regatta in Catalina this weekend," he told me.

"Yes, I was supposed to go, but since my boat's in the shop, I think I'm gonna miss it. I was really looking forward to it."

"My partner and I are going." He didn't look at me when he said this. Was this an invitation?

"No kidding! Oh, I'm so jealous. It's gonna be such a blast."

"You know, you can take a boat over to Catalina from Long Beach," he informed me. That definitely didn't sound like an invitation.

"Oh, yes, I know," I said, "but it's just not the same."

"Well, everything looks okay down here. We should have the lab work back in a couple weeks, and we'll let you know if anything comes out irregular."

"It shouldn't. I haven't had sex in a while. Anyway, thanks again. I didn't feel a thing." I considered telling him that it was the best Pap smear I had ever had, but I didn't want to overdo it.

"Who were you planning on going over to Catalina with?" he asked as he was about to open the door to leave.

"Oh, a girlfriend of mine. We go all the time."

"Well, if you girls are in a bind, I'd be glad to give you a lift to the island. It's nothing too exciting, just me and Dr. Wheeler, but a patient in need..."

"Oh, I'd hate to impose," I said.

"Oh, please, you might be doing us a favor. It'll be nice to have someone aboard who knows how to sail instead of me. Dr. Wheeler isn't the most gifted seaman." I wasn't sure if I wanted to make this kind of commitment, but Dr. Luke was getting sexier and the thought of seeing him in a pair of shorts with his hair blowing in the wind made me shiver.

"That would be amazing," I said. "Do you really think it would be okay?"

"Sure. It will be fun to have some young company. I'll leave my number at the front for you. Call me this week and we'll set it up."

"That's so awesome of you! Thank you!"

I couldn't believe how nice this guy was. That was so easy. Except for the part about me sailing.

I also had to figure out which girlfriend of mine was deserving enough of a weekend trip to Catalina with a doctor. Ivory would be very jealous, but she would have to lie in the bed she made for me. I got Dr. Luke's number at the front desk and hurried outside to find the nearest bookstore. I needed to pick up a copy of *Sailing for Dummies* fast.

My phone rang while I was driving. It was my best friend from high school, Rory. She had gone to Penn after high school, gotten an undergrad degree in psychology, and then moved to L.A. to pursue a career in acting and had instead pursued one guy after another. "I need to get out of my date Friday with that loser anesthesiologist. I asked him if he would anesthetize me the other night, and he looked at me as if I asked him to fuck me in the eye. I can't bear another dinner with this guy."

"Just tell him you're going to Catalina for the weekend with your new gynecologist boyfriend."

"I wish," she said.

"No, really. We're going to Catalina this weekend with my new gyno and his partner."

"Are you being serious?" she asked.

"Yes. On a sailboat."

"I love you."

"Thank you. I didn't actually get a look at your guy, but he is a doctor."

"Do they have access to anesthesia?"

"One would assume."

"Please tell me these arrangements were made while he was giving you a breast exam."

"I can one-up that."

"You make me so happy; I'll call you right back."

Rory and I met our studs at his boat slip in the marina. Dr. Wheeler's name was Matthew. He was no Dr. Luke, but he was cute in a darker, more mysterious way. Rory immediately thought Dr. Luke was for her but I told her to step off.

The boat was beautiful. It was huge and white with massive sails. I knew for sure I couldn't pretend to sail it. I had brought plenty of booze along to give myself a good excuse, but apparently I didn't have to worry because another couple had been invited and they were "avid sailors." Dr. Luke told me that if I wanted in on any of the action I was going to have to take a stand; his friends Lori and Glen were very controlling at the helm of a boat.

"Oh, well, we'll just see about that," was my response.

An hour into our boat ride, Dr. Luke pulled out a bag full of Ecstasy. A drug-toting gynecologist! I had died and gone to heaven. When he asked us if we partied, I thought Rory may have peed in her pants a little. Matthew warned us to keep it on the down-low because Lori and Glen didn't "party."

We all popped our tabs and wandered onto the deck. The thought occurred to me that this was possibly the happiest day of my life. Rory and Matthew started an intense conversation about religion and life on other planets. Those two topics were about as interesting to me as the Louisiana Purchase, so I just bided my time and waited for an in to the conversation.

The more Matthew talked and drank, the more I got the impression that something was definitely wrong with him. I couldn't quite put my finger on it. I kept glancing at Dr. Luke for his reaction, but he was barely paying attention to me. Maybe I didn't look so good, I worried. But I knew that was impossible. I had had a facial and a haircut that morning. I'd have to be Tarzan to not look good at that point. During one of Matthew's stories, Rory leaned in and whispered, "He's hot." I was thinking the exact opposite but instead nodded encouragingly and said, "I know, see if you can get him alone."

Getting him alone, however, seemed impossible. Matthew was going on and on about how sometimes he can see his dead relatives, not really leaving much room for me and

Dr. Luke to get to know each other any better. I needed to talk to Dr. Luke and charm him, so he would start paying more attention to me, but he didn't seem interested at all.

We were on our third bottle of Veuve Clicquot when Matthew said he had to "hit the head." Finally, I would get some stage time. I could talk about my theory of dwarfism and how I think there is an undeniable connection between them and the Little Dipper. It wouldn't be long before Dr. Luke realized that I was more than just a pretty face.

"I'm going down below to get us some cheese and crackers," Dr. Luke said and left. Two seconds later, Rory stood up. "I'm going downstairs to have sex with Matthew," she said.

The Ecstasy was starting to kick in, but unlike the rest of the human race, Ecstasy doesn't make me horny. Sure, I may want to kiss someone, but the sudden and rabid need for sex doesn't happen. I much prefer to sit outside, look at the stars, and daydream about what life would have been like had I become a professional women's basketball player.

I told Rory I didn't care what she did as long as she left me alone, because I was starting to feel really good. About five minutes later, she came back and grabbed my arm, a flurry of delight on her face.

"You're flying," I said.

"Yeah, and I'm not the only one. Come with me."

"Leave me here, go, you can have him," I mumbled. I would have been perfectly happy if I never saw another person again in my life. I felt amazing.

"The guys are waiting for us," Rory said.

"Where?" I asked.

"Downstairs. Come on, Chelsea!"

"Okay."

I got up and walked downstairs with her. As we approached the bedroom, I heard a very recognizable sound coming from behind the door—only to be followed by seeing a very shocking thing when Rory pushed open the door. Matthew was inside Dr. Luke. He was doing him doggie style, holding down his head and smacking his ass. What was happening? I wanted to run over and protect Dr. Luke's honor, but he seemed to be enjoying himself. Also, I was a little thrown. I had never seen two men having sex before in real life. Rory just stood beside me with a huge grin on her face. She loved controversy.

I had so many different emotions running through me that I was frozen in place. The only thing I could do was to shout, "Stop that!"

Matthew and Dr. Luke both looked over at me with huge Ecstasy smiles on their faces and kept going.

"What is going on here?" I demanded. I sounded like my father.

Rory was enjoying every minute of my mortification. She didn't even lower her voice to say, "Turns out they're both gay."

"No, he's his *partner*," I said.

"Yes, Chelsea...get it?"

"Oh, shit." I finally realized what kind of partner he was talking about. I couldn't believe it. I was too high to deal with this. I told Rory we needed to swim to shore.

We ran up onto the deck and asked Lori and Glen where the life jackets were. Rory asked them how long before we got to Catalina. They said we'd be there in about twenty minutes. Great. No problem. We'd rent a hotel room and take a boat back tomorrow.

I told Rory not to blow our high and we'd have fun no matter what. The important thing was not to think about what was happening or what I had just seen. I had to focus on the positive—whatever that was. Rory grabbed four more tabs of Ecstasy and shoved them in her purse.

"Good thinking," I said.

Dr. Luke and Matthew came upstairs just as we were docking. They were all over each other. It was painful to watch, like seeing your boyfriend cheat on you but with a man. Rory, however, couldn't stop laughing, and eventually I started laughing too, and then *they* both started laughing. Then they headed toward us with very lascivious looks in their eyes. Dr. Luke reached for my boob and asked if I wanted to get it from two guys at once. "That was sooo five years ago," I thought about saying. Instead I said, "Look at the stars."

Rory told them that she wasn't into getting it in the ass and that we were leaving once the boat docked.

"We didn't ask you," Dr. Luke said.

"Excuse me?" asked Rory, offended.

Quickly, I told them we'd love to hang out more, but we were meeting friends and had to fly. No pun intended.

Once we got off the boat we took another tab and had a blast trying to find a hotel. We kept getting distracted by the sky. After a while, I needed water badly so we stopped at a bar—only to find about 150 swing dancers in mid-prance. The bartender told us that Catalina was having its annual swing-dancing convention. I couldn't believe there was such a thing. He warned us that every hotel was booked. We had only one option at that point, and that was to get in on the fun. So we swing danced well into the wee hours of the morning, with the help of our additional Ecstasy tabs, and when the lights were shut off, we went to the beach and watched the sun come up. We hadn't done that since prom. We caught the first ferry back to Long Beach and took a taxi to Santa Monica. In the cab, Rory told me I had lost my touch since high school. I reminded her that I was their first pick for a gang bang. That shut her up.

Ivory was very disappointed when I gave her the bad news. She went back to her old gynecologist and so did I. But a few months later, I ran into Dr. Luke at Jerry's Famous Deli in the marina. I was with a guy I was dating, and Dr. Luke was with the biggest black man I had ever seen. Just the sight of the two of them together made my anus tighten. I noticed Dr. Luke making his way over to my table, so I got up and walked in the other direction, straight to my car. I couldn't afford a run-in with this guy in front of my new suitor. There were only three things he could bring up: my vagina, his anus, and his Ecstasy that I stole.

I called my date on his cell phone and asked him to meet me outside. I explained that this guy was a lunatic and he was always harassing me and I couldn't bear to have a conversation with him.

"He seemed pretty normal," my guy said. "He asked if your boat was out of the shop yet. I didn't know you had a boat."

OH, SHUT UP ALREADY!

ONE OF MY best friends in the world is Shoniqua. She is black. She's also six feet tall and has an ass the size of a medicine ball. I call her "Hammer Toes."

Shoniqua is the only person I know who can actually make me look shy. She has a huge personality. She can walk into a room full of people and within seconds take over. When I'm with her I just sit back, relax, and enjoy the show.

We've been friends for ten years, and all the while she has been with the same man—married to him for the last five. He is a true African, from Nigeria, who I'm pretty sure is capable of Voodoo. He'll take one look at someone and before even speaking to them decide that they are no good for Shoniqua. I was scared when I met him because I knew my insides were flooded with alcohol and I was sure he would take that as a bad sign. Fortunately for me he thought I was a good seed, just confused about where my life was headed. His analysis sounded a lot better than being a "slut," so we grew to be fast friends too.

I met Shoniqua while I was performing stand-up comedy at some hole-in-the-wall coffee shop in Alta Dena. She ran a comedy room filled with only black performers and black audiences. She wasn't opposed to whiteys coming to patronize or perform, but this wasn't a section of town with a surplus of Caucasians.

I knew that Shoniqua's place was the perfect platform for my comedy. Black audiences always seemed to have a better sense of humor than white ones. Their laughter is hard to get, but once you have it, they really let go. I enjoy challenges, and so the next step in my comedy career was to ingratiate myself with the brotherhood.

The first person I met at the club was Shoniqua's mother, who also happened to be black. When her mother questioned why a blond, blue-eyed Jewish girl would make her way to that part of town, I wrote her a check for one hundred dollars and asked her to please be nice to me. She took the check and told me to buy her a Corona. Why they sold Corona at a coffee shop was unclear to me, but as the person behind the counter pulled an ice-cold Corona from a portable beach cooler, I realized businesses in this neighborhood were clearly subject to different regulations.

I was extremely nervous before going onstage but the set ended up going well, thanks to a 350-pound black woman who hooted and hollered at every joke I told. There weren't many people in the audience, and I couldn't hear anyone laugh over this woman, but I decided it had been a positive experience and asked Shoniqua if I was allowed to come back. She told me that she liked white people but didn't have any close white friends and asked if I was interested in cross-pollinating. I told her we would see how things went but not to put the chicken wing before the egg.

We grew to be fast friends, and a couple years later we made plans for a weekend getaway to the Big Apple.

We booked separate rooms at the Peninsula Hotel because Shoniqua didn't like sharing a room. I, on the other hand, love sharing rooms with anyone, especially girls. It reminds me of childhood sleepovers, where you would talk into the wee hours of the morning and put the fingers of the girl who fell asleep first into hot water to make her pee in her sleep. I did this once to Shoniqua, but it wasn't as much fun without anyone else there to witness it. The next morning, when she realized what had happened, Shoniqua came very close to bitch slapping me. She was physically superior to me in strength and I had to outmaneuver her for almost thirty minutes. With her long arms and legs coming at me from every direction, it felt like I was fending off a real live octopus. It took a while before she would speak to me again after that. Reluctantly, I agreed that all future trips together would be in separate rooms. I was not happy about it, but I was working my way back into her circle of trust.

On the second night of our trip to Manhattan, the concierge told us about a great new restaurant called Tao. He tried to make us a reservation but it was completely booked, so Shoniqua took over.

She called the restaurant and informed the hostess that we were the executive producers of the television show *Friends* and that there was a possibility Monica and Chandler would be joining us. I reminded her that those were not their actual names, but she was already hanging up the phone. "We're in," she said.

"Oh, really?" I asked. "And where do you suppose we're going to find Monica and Chandler?"

"Listen, bitch. They're not gonna fuckin' care when we get there."

She was right. They didn't care. But they did take a long hard look at two twenty-seven-year-olds, wondering how it was possible we were the executive producers of anything beyond a half-hour segment on the Nickelodeon channel. I kept my head down and avoided eye contact with anyone. Shoniqua, however, milked it for all it was worth.

"Hello, nice to see you this evening. Is our table ready?" she said with a big cheesy grin that reminded me of a billy goat in heat.

When we were seated, she told the hostess, "Please make sure we get a complimentary round of drinks. We had a long flight. I'd love something sweet."

"That's okay," I told the hostess. "Just ignore her."

"Fuck off, ho!" Shoniqua snapped at me, then looked up at the hostess and sternly commanded, "Just ignore *her*."

The hostess gave us an uncomfortable smile and walked off.

"Cut the shit," I said. "Why do you have to be so embarrassing?"

"Listen, bitch, they don't know who the fuck we are; let's get some free shit. I'm not a Jew like you, okay." Shoniqua thought being a Jew meant that I was born with a trust fund and received direct deposits into my account from the Bank of Abraham. I explained to her, on many occasions, that my family was the Sanford and Son of our neighborhood and the only trust fund my father had in store for me was a 1985 Yugo with a missing radiator. She chose to ignore this information and instead focus on the fact that we had a summer home.

The dinner was fantastic. I introduced her to foie gras, along with Kobe steak and yellowtail sashimi. Shoniqua was a walking oxymoron: She never bought a handbag or a pair of sunglasses that wasn't Prada, Gucci, or Chanel, but she couldn't pronounce filet mignon or, for that matter, pick it up with a pair of chopsticks. I'm not the most sophisticated girl in the world, but my brother Ray is a chef, and it didn't take me long to figure out what was worth eating and what was worth skipping for more alcohol.

Shoniqua and I always had a great time when we went out, and this night was no different. She was regaling me with a story about one of the 107 children her mother fostered when, out of the corner of my eye, I spotted my hot piece of Peruvian ass.

He was at the bar, leaning up against a glass partition, watching us. He was tall, with olive skin and wavy black hair. His nose was a little crooked but not enough to ruin his face.

I told Shoniqua that there was a beautiful specimen right behind her but not to look right away. "Heeeeeeeeeeeey!" she screamed in what she thought was a flirty tone and knocked on the glass like we had been dropped onto the wrong side of an aquarium. The billy goat was back.

Every person within twenty feet of our table was now staring in our direction. "Hey there!" she shouted, rapping on the glass again. I slid lower in my seat and contemplated using my dirty napkin as a burka. Shoniqua is great for introductions to new men since she is married and doesn't give a shit what anyone of the opposite sex thinks. "I *got* a husband," she would tell me if I ever asked her to tone it down. "I'm fucking trying to get one for your ass too." Shoniqua and her husband have the greatest relationship I know of; I can only assume it's because they don't have kids. They're constantly surprising each other with weekend getaways and showering each other with gifts. They talk on the phone close to ten times a day. Lately I've realized I need a man just like him for myself. Except white.

Men love Shoniqua's straightforwardness and always seem to be charmed by her. She's a great partner in crime because I don't have to do much except be humiliated. We had perfected our "one-two punch" technique on several occasions. Shoniqua would talk to my prey about religion, their homeland, and her husband who was a banker. I would jump in every once in a while to reinstate my position as his future sexual partner, commenting about how National Geographic's exposés on the wild were starting to look more and more like an episode of *CSI: Miami*.

"Here he comes," Shoniqua said. "Try not to fuck this up."

My Latin lover rounded the corner and took a seat next to Shoniqua. He was at least six feet tall, with dark brooding eyes and a flirty half smile. I knew for sure I had to have sex with him.

"Hello, ladies," he said in his Antonio Banderas accent.

I don't know what it is about accents that makes me want to get undressed and high-five myself. I'm helpless against any accent—except a British one. My ex-boyfriend's British accent was charming for the first two months, mostly because I couldn't understand a word he said. (It was very similar to the *Crocodile Hunter* guy. The first two episodes, you're thinking, This guy is great! Two more episodes and you want to dress up like an alligator and bite his hand off.) After the initial honeymoon phase wore off with my ex, I was ready to scream, "Stop talking like that, damnit. Talk like me. Just try!" Not a fair trade for someone who wasn't even circumcised. I've never understood why they don't circumcise men in European countries; most of them end up here, anyway.

My little Don Juan's accent was sexy and thick. At times, his words were barely decipherable. But this may also have been due to my failing eardrums, which were aligning with my failing liver, which was, no doubt, wondering why I had to keep torturing it. "Liver," I would say, "you only live once, or at least I do, and you should be grateful to be along for the ride."

He was visiting New York from Peru, where he worked as a mechanical engineer. That didn't interest me as much as my visions of him capturing anacondas on the Amazon, so I chose to stick with that mental picture instead.

He kept making eyes at me while Shoniqua and he were chatting, which was sweet and reassuring since we would be the ones having sex. In her characteristic and persuasive way, Shoniqua mostly dominated the conversation. She found out that this was his first trip to the States, and his name was Lupé. I had always believed that Lupé was short for Guadelupé, which is, I thought, a woman's name. To avoid bringing this up in conversation, and thus postpone the moment when people would just stare at me with disappointment in their eyes, I excused myself from the table to take a breather.

I went outside to bum a cigarette. On the corner, just beyond the door, I saw another adorable face. My seven margaritas instantly took over. "Hey, you. Come over here. Will you come inside with me and pretend you're my boyfriend? There's a guy at our table who won't leave and I want him to think I'm taken," I lied. It was time to bring in reinforcements. I had to let Lupé know what a hot piece of real estate I was.

I shimmied back to the table, holding hands with my new boyfriend.

I sat down next to Lupé and made the introductions. Shoniqua glared at me and kicked me under the table with one of her massive feet. Meanwhile, I was looking back and forth between my two options, trying to figure out who was cuter. My new boyfriend didn't have an accent and looked about twenty-one. My Peruvian still had his accent and looked about thirty-five. Then the newbie mentioned being a rave promoter and the battle was over. "Are they still doing those?" I asked. I hadn't been to a rave since I was eleven, and from what I remember, staying up dropping acid until six in the morning was no walk in the park. I figured I would be better off with La Bamba.

I told the young boy to scram, as he had nobly fulfilled his commitment to me.

Lupé said he was going to the bathroom. To ensure he'd come back, I asked him if he wanted another drink. He requested a whiskey on the rocks. I've never bought into the whole soul mate thing, but after hearing this guy order the one thing I love to see a man drink, I considered getting my tarot cards read.

"Who the fuck was that other guy, you shithead?" blasted Shoniqua. "Now you're just getting cocky."

"Sorry, I'm drunk."

"Listen, I'm sitting here slaving over this fuckin' guy trying to get you some booty, and you're running around cockblocking your fuckin' self. He likes your skinny monkey ass, I don't fuckin' know why, but he does, so don't do anything stupid." I bit my tongue. Not on purpose. I actually bit my tongue.

"Ow, shit, I just bit my—"

"Shut up. Here he comes. Hiiiiiiiiiiiiiiiiiii!" squealed Shoniqua. "Lupé, you ready to get out of here? I've got a jammin' party for us to go to," she said with more enthusiasm than a QVC representative after a six-pack of Red Bull.

One of Shoniqua's friends was releasing his new hip-hop album and we were scheduled to attend the party. Ordinarily, it would have been fun, but I definitely wasn't going to let Lupe see me dancing next to black people.

"Why don't we stop by the hotel and freshen up?" I said, giving her the "pay attention" stare.

"Okay, okay, sure," she said, catching on.

We got the check and Lupé offered to put in some money, but I wouldn't think of it, considering what I had in store for him. "You can pay for me too, bitch," Shoniqua said. I'd have had to be Helen Keller not to have seen that one coming.

As we stood up to leave, Shoniqua whispered to me, "It's taken care of, you're gettin' it, and I'm going to the party without you."

"Fine," I said. "Just pretend you're coming back to the room to get us, so it doesn't seem so obvious." I always assumed anyone with an accent was automatically slow on the uptake, when in actuality the only one a few pom-poms short of a pep rally was me.

The three of us climbed into a cab, with Lupé in the middle. I turned and said, "I think you're *really* gonna love America."

"Copy that," Shoniqua said.

"Two such beautiful women, I am very lucky," Lupé said.

"Well, Lupé, *that's just how we fuckin' roll,*" Shoniqua said.

When we got back to the hotel, we bid adieu to Shoniqua and I asked Lupé to come up with me to my room. Once inside the elevator, he said, "We are not going to the party right away, are we?"

"We're actually not going to the party at all," I replied.

He had a big smile on his face and I was glad he was happy with this decision. "I was hoping to get some time alone with you, to talk," he said, gazing at me with his big bedroom eyes. "You were very quiet at dinner. But you have beautiful smile..." He hesitated. It seemed as if he was searching for the right words to say. I didn't have all night, so I made my first move.

We were making out in the elevator and it was hot—just like in the movies. And it was a pretty nice elevator too. I had never had sex in an elevator, and this seemed like the perfect opportunity.

"Do you have a condom?" I whispered in between kisses.

"A who?" he asked.

"A condom...protection."

"Oh," he said, "no, no, no, I do not own condom."

This was very cute to me.

"It's okay," I said. "We can run out and buy some."

He stopped kissing me and held my face in his hands. "I would rather spend the evening with you talking and having nice time. No condom necessary." He paused and then followed it up with, "I don't feel comfortable spending our first night...together."

"Listen, Lupé," I said, "this is our *last* night! Don't get your hopes up. It's cold and I'm tired, so get out that piñata and let's get this party started."

I didn't understand what was happening. This had never happened to me before. I had been denied sex on certain occasions, sure, but they usually involved a three a.m. phone call.

"You are upset, are you not?" he asked.

Upset? I was stark-raving mad. I couldn't understand why a traveling man would come to the United States and not jump at the opportunity to be manhandled by an American girl.

I knew that I couldn't physically overpower Lupé, but there was a chance of him losing some strength after a couple more drinks. I wasn't a huge fan of being on top, but desperate times called for desperate measures, and it looked like I was going to have to ride him like a pony.

"I'm not upset," I told him, "not at all. That's very sweet. Let's go have some drinks in my room."

I got a water glass from the bathroom and poured Lupé a nice long whiskey straight from the minibar. "Let's do a shot," I said.

We started kissing again, standing up, and then fell onto the bed. After a good thirty seconds, I reached for his penis, but he stopped me. "Slow down, slow down," he said.

This guy was really pissing me off. What was the story? I appreciated the idea of taking our time *in bed,* but not beforehand. After I got him naked, I would gladly roll around for hours if that was what he wanted.

"Are you seriously not going to have sex with me?" I asked.

He pulled me to him into a sort of cuddling position that suspiciously felt like a full nelson.

This guy was gonna drive me to drink...more. I lost my steam, grabbed the remote control, and found the Animal Planet channel.

The next hour consisted of us snuggling and watching eight morons compete in different challenges with animals. I had heard about men getting blue balls before, but didn't know it could happen to a female. At that very moment, my vagina was turning a deep shade of navy.

"Do you want to go to that party?" I asked him.

"Not really, this is nice," he said and burrowed his face into my shoulder.

This guy was a *hot* mess. Who on earth behaved like this? What was the point of traveling if you wanted to sit in hotel rooms and watch TV? He must have grown up in the wild, with no civilization at all, to think *this* was a good time. I was struggling to come up with ways to get him to leave, but I was too exhausted. I tried to fart, but nothing came out. Then he started to snore.

I fell asleep shortly after I resigned myself to the idea that I was, in fact, sharing a bed with someone who wouldn't put out. This was not the ending I had envisioned for the evening. Instead of steamy South American sex, the entire night was spent with Lupé holding on to me for dear life like a koala bear to a tree branch. Being cuddled while awake is nice, but when I'm sleeping, I need space. I kept waking up every hour, trying to nudge him toward the other side of the bed, but he slept like a big dead log. My shoulder started to ache from lying on my side, but there wasn't any other choice; whenever I turned around all I got was hot breath in my face. I was close to tears and thought about calling hotel security, but I didn't want Lupé to end up in the clinker.

At around seven a.m. I picked up the hotel telephone, went into the bathroom, and called myself on my cell, which I had placed next to Lupé's head with the ringer on high. I ran out of the bathroom in a fit of panic to answer my cell and saw his eyes open slightly. "Hello?" I answered inquisitively. "Oh, no, we do? Oh, of course, I'm just, I'm just aaaah...okay, I'll be here." I hung up. "Shit!" I screamed.

Lupé bounced up. "What is it?"

"I have a meeting in ten minutes, and it's in this room. You're gonna have to go. I am sooooo sorry."

"It's okay, it's okay, what kind of meeting is it?" he asked.

I wasn't prepared for his English to work first thing in the morning and was thrown off guard by the question.

"It's with the manager of this hotel, actually. Shoniqua and I are thinking about buying it."

"Oh, I didn't know you were into real estate. Shoniqua told me you were a professional ballerina."

This was news to me. "I am...a ballerina...but I also buy buildings...hotels mostly...and then fix them up and sell them." I said this with about as much believability as Pamela Anderson as a lifeguard.

"Oh, okay...when do you think you'll be done?"

"It's gonna be a long one," I said. "Why don't you give me your cell number and I'll call you tonight."

"I thought maybe we could go to the zoo today," he said.

This came as no surprise to me, considering his affinity for things in captivity. "Probably not, but I'll call you later," I said. He told me he had no cell phone and asked for my number. I gave him Shoniqua's.

He got dressed and came over to kiss me good-bye, grabbing my face for what felt like an hour. He just kept staring into my eyes. "I had a beautiful time last night."

"Yeah, it was a real hoot," I said.

After he left, I locked the door, slept for another three hours, then put on a robe and went straight to Shoniqua's room.

"What's up?" she asked as she opened the door.

"What's up? What's up? Not Lupé's penis, that's for fucking sure."

"What happened?" she asked.

I got into bed with her and told her about my night of torture. "Well, bitch, that's what you get when you fuck with a sister and make her piss herself."

"Huh? What do you mean?"

"Think about it, Magnum P.I.," she said, with a big smile on her face. "You white bitches aren't the only ones who can plan some shit. I told Lupé that you only had three months to live and that this trip was our last hoorah. I explained that you had been treated terribly by men in the past and your dying wish was to be adored emotionally, not sexually." She paused and added, "I also told him you had herpes." Then she burst into maniacal, uncontrollable laughter.

"That's not fucking funny," I kept saying, all the while trying to control my own laughter. When I couldn't any longer, I decided to go up to my room and laugh in private. I refused to give her the satisfaction of seeing me entertained by my pathetic circumstance.

"Fuck off," I yelled as I left her room. "By the way, he wants to go to the zoo today!" I shouted as the door swung shut.

Lupé called Shoniqua several times after our trip to New York to check on my status. "I'll be honest with you, Lupé," she said on their last call, "it doesn't look good. It doesn't look fucking good."

A Wedding Story

I WAS ON the phone with my doctor's office trying to get my hands on some Vicodin.

"What do you need it for?" the nurse who answered asked.

"I'm in a lot of pain," I lied. "I had a bit of bad luck over the weekend."

"I'm sorry to hear that, but you'll need to be more specific, Ms. Handler."

"Fine," I said. "If you must know, I was skydiving and my chute didn't open."

"Oh dear god, are you all right?" she asked me.

"Yes, I'm okay, I'm just in a lot of pain," I told her.

"What...where...how did you land?" the nurse asked me.

"In a tree," I said.

"Have you been to the hospital? Is anything broken or bruised?" she asked me.

"No, it's mostly internal injuries, nothing you'd be able to spot externally. I also feel like I'm suffering from post-traumatic syndrome, so I may need some sleeping pills."

My call-waiting beeped and I told the nurse to hold the wire.

It was my sister Sloane, whose wedding was two months away.

"You can bring a guest to the wedding if you want," she said.

"Hold on," I said and clicked back over to find that the nurse had hung up on me.

I clicked back to Sloane. "Fine. Who?" I asked her.

"I don't know. One of your girlfriends or if you meet a guy you want to bring."

The thought of bringing a love interest to my sister's wedding had about as much allure as joining the Navy SEALs. Every time I brought someone home to meet my parents, whether it was just a friend or an actual boyfriend, my family felt compelled to remind me that I had terrible taste in people and that they liked me better when flying solo. They all agreed that my friends in California were shallow and brain-dead and we were all much better off when I left them behind.

My Mormon sister was engaged to a normal human, and it seemed he was helping her to slowly snap out of the spell the Mormons had put her under. Sloane's wedding was being held at our summerhouse in Martha's Vineyard. Though I had recently been out a couple times with a guy I liked, I didn't want to embarrass myself on our third date by asking him to fly across the country for my sister's wedding.

Since my gay friend Nathan had included me in many of his family events and vacations, it seemed like time for a little reciprocity. My father had never met a gay man in person before and I thought that this could be a time of great revelation. Once again, I was sorely mistaken.

For the record, Nathan is not your typical gay man. He's not as blatant a homosexual as Harvey Fierstein, but if you have any gaydar at all—which I don't—then it wouldn't take you more than a couple of nights out with Nathan to catch on.

I didn't realize he was gay for a long time, attributing most of his effeminacy and idiosyncratic ways to the fact that he is Jewish. He is tall and handsome, a sports fanatic, and a man's man in many ways—except when having a verbal disagreement, in which case he turns into an eight-year-old girl.

Nathan and I have been friends for many years. I met Nathan when I was nineteen years old and landed my first job waiting tables at Morton's, a restaurant in Los Angeles. He trained me on my first day, and when I spilled a glass of red wine on some woman who had more eye liner on than Liza Minnelli, he assured me that big things were in the cards for me.

Bringing Nathan home, however, was not quite the stroke of genius I had anticipated. Minutes after introducing Nathan to my mother, he sat down at our kitchen table and told my mom how famished he was from the trip. "What can I make you, sweetheart?" she asked. "We've got cold cuts, potato salad, I can heat up some chili..."

"I'll take four eggs over medium, absolutely no oil or butter. I'll also take a turkey sandwich on multigrain with some mustard—Dijon if you have it."

I wasn't sure what to make of Nathan's behavior but felt that I needed to defend my mother.

"Is that all, or would you also like her to whip you up a brisket with some gravy?" I said.

"Oh, I'm sorry," he said. "I'm so hungry I can't even think."

"Chelsea," my mother said in a disapproving tone. "Don't be silly, it's my pleasure," she lied.

My brother Greg walked into the living area still in boxer shorts and a T-shirt, yawning and scratching the back of his neck. That's when our dog Whitefoot and my father, who was wearing a Sean John tracksuit and Uggs, came in through the sliding glass door that leads to the back deck. That's also when Nathan began to squeal like a pig.

"Oh, my goodness, look at this beautiful creature," he said, running over toward Whitefoot. He dropped to both knees and began petting him uncontrollably. "Yes, yes, you like that, you big beast of a doggie dog dog, don't you? Do you like it? Yes you do, you do do do do do! I love you already, yes I do, yes I do. Do you love me? I think you do!" Whitefoot's tail was wagging and he was maniacally licking Nathan, whose mouth was also open. It didn't take much to get Whitefoot aroused and I knew that his miniature ding-a-ling was at full throttle.

"What a gorgeous creature!" Nathan cooed, in a voice that a mother would use to talk to an infant. Whitefoot's your basic mutt, with the ability to sit when commanded—a sweet dog but nothing to go crazy over. Nathan was not a flamboyant guy and I had never seen him act like this before.

My father eyed this exchange with disgust. Then he loudly cleared his throat. We were not off to a good start. Greg, meanwhile, looked on with a huge smile on his face. He loved watching our dad's reaction to anyone left of center. After allowing Whitefoot to face-rape him for another ten seconds, Nathan stood up and approached my father with open arms. My father took a step back and put out his hand instead.

Greg had met Nathan before on a visit to Los Angeles and gave him a bear hug.

"This is gonna be fantastic," Greg said to me on his way into the kitchen.

Once Nathan had finished eating the small feast my mother had prepared for him, he asked which room was his and then promptly changed into his running clothes. It was early afternoon and everyone was at the beach, so our normally chaotic house filled with my five siblings, their significant others, and their half a dozen kids was empty and unusually quiet.

I gave Nathan directions on where to go on his run, opting to stay home to do some damage control.

As the front door shut and Nathan took off on his run, my father looked up from reading the newspaper. He glared at me, his reading glasses resting low on his nose.

"Well, looks like Chelsea brought home another loose cannon," he said to my mother.

I needed to change the subject quickly for fear my father's already tenuous good mood would get worse, so I asked him if the gardener was done preparing the lawn for the wedding.

"Yeah, he's done," my father said, disinterested. "I told him to take one of those linden trees as his payment."

"What?" my mother asked.

"Those linden trees. We've got two of them and they're normally found in Germany. Very rare."

"Melvin," my mother said, "how is he supposed to take one of our trees?"

"Simple," my father said. "All he has to do is cut it down and load it into a truck. It's not a big deal."

Greg's face lit up. He took major delight in all of my father's business maneuvers. He is of the thought that my father is wildly insane and operates on a completely different plane of existence.

"Why would the gardener want one of our trees?" Greg asked innocently.

"Those trees are very valuable, Greg. They're worth about fifteen hundred dollars. Who *wouldn't* want one is my question."

"Right," Greg said, "but is our gardener in the tree-selling business? A tree's not something you just take out into the marketplace and sell."

"Not sure," my father said and then went back to his newspaper.

"Well, when is he going to cut down the tree?" my mother asked.

"I don't know, he's gotta get some guys and rent a truck," he said.

"Well, not before the wedding, I hope," she said.

"Maybe if we're lucky he'll saw it down right in the middle of the wedding," Greg said.

"Nah, he wouldn't do that," my dad replied, as if my brother were serious.

"I wonder if there'll be a bidding war on eBay," Greg said.

"If he wants to sell it on eBay, let him sell it on eBay, what do I care? All I know is this guy's making out like a bandit!" my father said.

I went to my room, changed, and came downstairs to find my sister and her fiancé. They had been visiting some friends who were in town for the wedding.

"Look at that figure," my father said, upon seeing me in a bathing suit. "Hot stuff tonight!"

Then he nudged my sister and said, "Look at that hourglass figure. She's a heartbreaker, this one."

Sloane reacted with disgust, as she always did. "That's your daughter, Dad. You're not supposed to be complimenting her figure."

I disagreed. I like compliments and don't care who they come from. Besides, my dad was always singing our praises to the point of embarrassment, only to turn around the next minute and say something like, "Some women don't get married until they're in their forties."

"Dad's got a crush on you, and I think it's disgusting," Sloane said.

"I love all my daughters equally," he announced. "Each one is more beautiful than the next!"

"Yeah? Where am I in that lineup?" Sloane asked.

"At the beginning," I told her.

My dad turned to me. "You got a lot of chutzpah, love.

Men aren't always going to respond to that. You're one of those girls who could do it all by herself. Make a fortune, have a couple kids...build a house."

"Who is she supposed to have kids with, Dad?" Sloane asked.

"Whomever! That's what women are doing these days. She's one hell of a smart-ass, that sister of yours," he said to Sloane, then looked at me. "But you got a good head on your shoulders and a lot of men find that intimidating. That's why you tend to hang out with such basket cases like your friend Nathan there."

"Sloane, did you hear the news?" Greg asked.

"Yes," I chimed in, ignoring my father. "You don't have to pay the caterer tomorrow, you can just give her one of our trees. They're very rare."

The door swung open and Nathan walked back inside, dripping sweat from his run.

"This place is beautiful, God, Melvin, just beautiful," he said to my father. Then he spotted Sloane. "You must be Sloaney Baloney! Yippee!" he shrieked and ran over to embrace her.

My future brother-in-law slid out the back door as soon as he saw that a hug might be headed his way. My father lowered his paper an inch below his eyes, watching Nathan like a detective on a stakeout.

"Sylvia," Nathan said to my mother, "I'd love a smoothie."

"Hey, asshole," I whispered, "this isn't Jamba Juice."

"Chelsea, I heard that," my mother said. "I'd love to make a smoothie for Nathan."

"Well, then, you better make one for Whitefoot too," my father said and muttered something under his breath.

After taking a forty-minute shower, then dumping his running clothes on top of our laundry machine and asking my mother not to wash his shorts and shirt together, Nathan picked up our phone and went into the bedroom where all the little kids sleep.

I quickly slipped outside to the deck to avoid further discussion with my father. Half an hour later, when I came back inside, Nathan was having a loud argument with his bookie/lover, which my father was listening to through my sister's baby monitor that he held inches away from his ear. My father got up, grabbed me by my elbow, and dragged me into the kitchen.

"Do you know what a *schnorrer* is?" he asked me.

"Dad, what is your problem?" I said.

"It's Yiddish for mooch. That *faygeleh* friend of yours is the classic definition of a mooch, and I don't like it one bit. When is he gonna get off the goddamn phone? We've got a wedding to arrange for that Mormon sister of yours and there's no goddamm cell-phone reception. What kind of *mishegas* is this?" *Mishegas* is another Yiddish word, for bullshit. "Do you know he has a bookie? Where did this guy grow up, in the woods?"

"Let go of my elbow, Dad."

"I don't like it one bit. Now tell me the truth, is he delirious?" my father asked in all seriousness. That was my father's way of asking if Nathan was on drugs.

The truth of the matter was that Nathan did all kinds of drugs, but I couldn't imagine he would've gotten on a plane to my sister's wedding with an eight ball smuggled inside his rectum. And as far as I knew, he hadn't been doing anything but drinking prior to the wedding. Nathan's MO is to go on binges for weeks at a time but then clean up his act for a couple of months. When he *is* on a binge, Nathan has a habit of staying up all night, coked to the gills, and then calling me or one of our other friends at seven in the morning, when he will bring up subjects like why in the game of Monopoly, Baltic Avenue is cheaper than Ventnor, when really it is in a better location. There are also long gaps of silence—if you don't count the times when he's grinding his teeth, or the sound of his vertical blinds hitting each other as he stands by the window, looking for the cops. I always want to hang up but get scared he might swallow his tongue.

"Dad!" I protested innocently. "Nathan is not on drugs. Stop being like this. Be nice to him!" When my father doesn't like someone, you don't have to have ESP to figure it out. He has the subtlety of a sling blade; all it takes is one moment of direct eye contact. And while it might once have been fun to watch him get riled up, I had long surpassed the golden years of experiencing sheer and utter elation in disappointing my father. At around twenty-four I realized I was just chasing that initial high you get the first time you tell your father at the age of sixteen that you're pregnant and thinking about keeping it.

"Just keep him away from your mother and keep him away from Whitefoot," my father ordered. Greg entered the kitchen just as my father said this.

"Yes, Chelsea, I think that's a good idea. Unless, of

course, Whitefoot brought condoms," Greg said. My father hates my brother's sense of humor even more than he hates mine. He looked at us both with disgust and headed for some bushes. "Oh look, Dad's going to relieve himself. That's charming," Greg said as we looked over and saw my father unzip his fly.

After Nathan got off the phone, I suggested we go to the beach. He said he'd rather sit on the deck and enjoy the view.

More of my family soon started funneling in, and I hoped that at least would take some of the attention off of Nathan. Luckily, my sister Sloane took a shine to him. He was giving her a ridiculous amount of compliments and Sloane was eating it up. If he wasn't complimenting her on her "piercing blue eyes," it was the way all her toes were the same length. This opened the door for her to ask him one question after another about being a member of GLAAD.

I was hoping my father would be charmed by Nathan, like most women were, but neither he nor any of my brothers wanted anything to do with him. I felt embarrassed for bringing him home and disappointing my family. The truth was, Nathan *was* behaving terribly. He was over the top about everything, and he was talking nonstop, barely letting anyone else get a word in edgewise. I kept trying to lure him outside, away from my father, but the more Nathan sensed he wasn't winning him over, the harder he put on a full-court press. When he wasn't praising my father about how lucky he was to have strong enough sperm to produce six healthy children, he was ordering food from my mother like he was in a twenty-four-hour diner. He had been there

for only one day and had already eaten close to six different meals, all of which he requested be prepared with absolutely no oil or butter.

"Why don't we go into town for a drink?" I offered,
steering Nathan, for the tenth time, toward the door. "Why
would we leave this paradise?" he said, breaking free of my
grip. "Everything we need is here."

"I don't know, Nathan, maybe because you're acting like
an asshole, and my mother isn't your personal chef."

"What are you talking about?"

"Just tone it down a notch, okay."

"Sloane loves me and so does Whitey. How can you say
that?"

"It's Whitefoot! And my parents don't give a shit who he
likes."

"You're being so dramatic!" he said and left me outside
by myself.

At around eight p.m., I had no other option but to dilute
two Tylenol PMs into his margarita. An hour later he was
in bed.

The next day was my sister's wedding, and Greg woke
me up to tell me that Nathan had already been on the phone
with his bookie for more than an hour.

"Now he's out on one of the kayaks taking a joyride.
And Dad's watching him with his binoculars. Dad could
have a meltdown at any minute," Greg said excitedly.

I rushed downstairs to the kitchen, where my mother
was making blueberry pancakes.

"Sweetie, I think you need to keep your friend Nathan
out of Dad's eye line when he comes back," my mother said.

"Your father is about to pass a kidney stone. I've made a list of last-minute items Nathan could pick up in town."

"Okay," I said. "Sorry, he's not usually like this."

My father walked in. "I'm not going to be able to hold my tongue for very much longer."

"Dad, please, I'm sorry. Do not say anything to him. He's had a rough life and his father used to hit him."

"For good reason!" my father said.

He popped a blueberry into his mouth. "Well, let's hope he'll kayak all the way back to California where he came from. Or if we're lucky, a heavy fog will roll in and he won't be able to find his way back. I need him out of my eye line. You picked a real winner there, Chelsea, a real one-two punch."

Obviously, my parents had had a conversation about my father's eye line.

"Why out of all your flaky friends in Los Angeles would you choose to bring a gay with you? Are you trying to tell us something?" he said as he playfully jabbed my side. "Our little Chelsea isn't a lesbian, is she?"

"No, Dad, I'm not a lesbian. I sleep with guys all the time," I replied and walked outside.

An hour later I was flat ironing my two-year-old niece's hair when Nathan entered the room, sweating profusely and reeking of tequila. "Sloane and I just rewrote her vows," he said.

"What are you talking about?" I asked.

"They were good, but they weren't great," he said. "I helped spice them up a bit."

"Are you drunk already? You stink of tequila."

"No, no, I'm fine. I just had a little shot," he told me. "Your father asked me to help set up the chairs for the ceremony. I think he likes me!"

It was time for all the bridesmaids to help Sloane get ready. After we got her dressed, she requested to be alone with Nathan before her walk down the aisle. While I was glad that someone in my family was responding positively to him, I wasn't clear about what kind of quick alliance they had formed, one so profound that it resulted in me not sharing the most important moment of my sister's life with her.

I went around our property checking on this and that and trying to keep my boobs in the dress my mother had sewn for me. She made each one of the bridesmaids a dress of the same material. I, of course, ended up being the only one who looked like a prostitute.

Being Mormon, Sloane had never used drugs and rarely drank alcohol. So it was clear to anyone who knew her that as she staggered down the aisle, she was intoxicated. Her new vows included lines from three different Grateful Dead songs. After she said, "And you're so smart, you could've been a school book," my sister Sidney whispered in my ear, "What the hell is she talking about?"

Once the ceremony had ended, we had a receiving line on the deck that faced the water. Sloane hoisted a glass of champagne, spilling some onto the ground. My father intercepted. He grabbed the glass, went inside, and poured it into Whitefoot's bowl. Then he ordered me to get some sparkling cider instead.

When the reception was under way, I found my table and sat next to Nathan.

Nathan winked and pointed between his legs. He had stolen a bottle of Cuervo from the bartender and hid it under our table where he could get to it quicker. Apparently the twenty-foot walk to the bar was too long a haul for him—and he didn't want to miss a beat hitting on my straight cousin sitting next to him. My cousin Neil, who was in from New York, politely excused himself and took his name place card with him.

Nathan was perspiring like a professional wrestler by the time he ordered his third lobster from the waitress. "What are you on?" I asked him. "You're dripping."

"Nothing, silly pickle! I'm just having a good time." I figured he'd be occupied with his bottle, so I got up to mingle. My father came over to me and asked if Nathan thought he was at Red Lobster.

"Listen, Dad, just ignore him. Have a good time. Look!" I pointed. "Sloane wants to dance with you."

Sloane and my dad hadn't been dancing for thirty seconds when Nathan shimmied onto the dance floor and cut in. I cleared three tables and the dance floor in just the amount of time needed to get Nathan out of my father's personal space.

"Cut the shit," I said through clenched teeth, while smiling for anyone watching. "Take a walk," I said. "A long one."

"I'd like to make a toast" were the next words out of Nathan's mouth.

He started clinking his glass of tequila with a knife. I shut my eyes in horror. "This is on behalf of me and Chelsea," he slurred.

My brother Greg yelled, "Let's hear it!" as the music and conversation came to a startling halt.

"I just want to say that I have never felt more welcome at somebody's house than I have at Mr. and Mrs. Handler's. This place is such a respite from my hectic and busy lifestyle in Hollywood where I produce music. I'm also interested in fitness. Anyway, there's nothing more beautiful than seeing a Mormon and a nonpracticing Christian come together at a Jewish gathering. All's fair in love and war."

Then he grabbed his bottle of tequila from under the table and stumbled away from the party.

About an hour later, mostly in fear of Whitefoot's safety, I walked around the property looking for Nathan to no avail. I *did* find Whitefoot. He was tied to a tree on the other side of the house, eating a lobster that my father, no doubt, had provided him with. Next to the lobster was a ramekin with melted butter for dipping.

At around eight p.m., when the party was winding down, I went into the basement to use the bathroom. That's where I found Nathan smoking pot with my thirteen-year-old cousin Kevin. He couldn't understand what was wrong with the situation and why I was being such a bitch.

I didn't understand how somebody could be so inappropriate at someone's parents' house. I had been Emily Post's alter ego when visiting Nathan's parents and never so much as swore in front of them, never mind consuming an entire bottle of tequila with no mixer. I proceeded to go off on him for close to five minutes, then grabbed my little cousin, took a hit of his joint, and started back up the stairs. I told Nathan he was not allowed out for the rest of the night, to which he inquired, "What about my lobster?" I went to our table, grabbed his plate with the lobster, and while descending the steps into the basement, took the lobster and threw it at him. He responded with a scream that sounded very similar to a cat getting gangbanged.

He woke up the next morning on the front lawn to my father spraying a hose on him.

"You're going to miss your flight," my father said. I was still so incensed at Nathan's behavior that I had Greg take him to the airport four hours early. When my brother returned, he announced to everyone in our living room with a huge grin on his face, "Well, have no fear, it looks like Robert Downey Junior got off without a hitch. We'll have to tune in to the local news later and see if his plane lands safely or if he ends up hijacking it."

"Shut up," I said. "He's not usually like that."

"I think we can all agree that Chelsea should not be allowed to bring anyone else back to any family gathering unless they are engaged to be married." My brother knew the chances of me getting engaged were about as probable as me releasing a hip-hop album.

My mother looked up from playing with my niece and said, "I think Greg is right, sweetheart. I think maybe when we have you all to ourselves it's more fun." My mother always put a spin on things to make it sound like every decision was based on how amazing you were to be around. I didn't want to bring anyone back there again, anyway. There was too much abuse from my siblings and father to endure another tandem vacation.

"You should really think about the company you keep," my father said. "You've got a real soft spot for lunatics. You're a beautiful girl, and I'd hate to see that figure go to waste."

OVERBOARD

DUMB DUMB ASKED me if I wanted to go on a cruise for New Year's Eve. I had never been on an ocean journey before and was hesitant because Dumb Dumb was about as much fun as a lawn bowling tournament. Her idea of a good time was going to California Pizza Kitchen and ordering two appetizers instead of one. But in my never-ending mission to get her twenty-eight-year-old hymen popped, I agreed.

"Just you and me will go," she said.

"No fucking way," I said. "I'm inviting Ivory and Lydia too."

"Fine," she said, "but they're not going to want to come with me."

She was right. Lydia and Ivory both told me they'd rather spend New Year's Eve at a Michael Bolton concert and that I was an idiot for having agreed to go in the first place. Upon hearing their totally rational refusals, I rethought my decision and tried to weasel my way out of the deal by telling Dumb Dumb I had a great opportunity to feed the homeless on New Year's and would have to cancel. An hour later I found Dumb Dumb crying in her room. I hate when people cry, especially when it's my fault, so not only did I agree to go with her, I ended up paying her way. Now who's the dumb dumb? I thought.

Right from the start, Dumb Dumb was way too excited about this trip. It's all she talked about for the next three weeks. She went on and on about the fun we were gonna have and all the hot men we would meet. I made her promise to at least let someone feel her boobs or I would tell everyone on board that she was still a virgin.

"You better not!" she yelled. "I'd kill you! Do you think I'll meet someone? Do you think I will? What if I meet my husband on the cruise ship? It's going to be so romantic!"

She would put on one fashion show after another in our apartment, modeling sarongs and different bikini tops.

"What do you think? Do you like the sarong with the polka dots or the one with the sun signs?"

She was exhausting. I was dreading this stupid cruise more than I had dreaded DUI school. It didn't help that Lydia and Ivory had made plans to go away to Aspen on a ski trip with Hugh Grant.

On her final runway walk, she modeled a bikini top with something that looked very similar to a pair of Dolphin shorts that were two sizes too small. If she walked around in that, I'd have to start calling her "Camel Toe."

"Listen, Camel Toe, I mean Dumb Dumb," I explained, "there are going to be a lot of opportunities on this cruise for you to meet someone, so I want you to prepare some conversation topics to bring up."

"I know how to talk to people, Chelsea," she responded.

This couldn't be further from the truth. The only people

Dumb Dumb could relate to were children and slow adults. And unless someone had watched every episode of *The Bachelor*, or TLC's *A Wedding Story*, Dumb Dumb was stumped for talking points. She watched reality shows over and over, and not just the original episodes but also reruns of the same episodes, and if TiVo didn't record something she had already seen, she would call her father to ask if he could somehow fix it from New Jersey. I had seen *The Bachelor* once and decided I wanted to do my own version of the show. It would involve me having sex with all the contestants and then eliminating them based on their penis size. Then, during my rose ceremony, I would wear some shimmery satin Nicole Miller design, preferably in eggplant, and I would say, "Leroy, Tyrone, and Jamal, will you accept these roses?"

I was not looking forward to this trip at all, and the closer we got to New Year's the better everyone else's plans sounded. "It's gonna be amazing, we're gonna meet so many guys," Dumb Dumb would say, ad nauseam.

"Shut up, already! You act like we're going to a man park. If you have high expectations you're only going to be disappointed," I told her. I had very *low* expectations and felt as if I was definitely going to be disappointed. Plus, I didn't know if I could handle this much alone time with Dumb Dumb. Her earnestness brought out a frightening violent side of me. I would try hard not to yell at her, but it was a constant challenge and I had never been stuck with her for more than a couple hours straight.

"Guess what? You are going to die!" Dumb Dumb exploded. She had just gotten back from the travel agent with our tickets. "It's a booze cruise and we're going to Ensenada!"

I was hoping I would never visit Ensenada again. It's not a place you need to see twice. I had been there a few years before on some overnight adventure with two guys I met at a bar the same night, and I remembered not eating for twenty-four hours. The whole city smelled bad and I'm not a big fan of buying blankets and parkas that have been lying on the pavement. I didn't understand the Mexicans' mentality and wondered how they could be so close to civilization and yet not know about the hard taco shell.

"It's a booze cruise!" she wailed again.

"You don't even drink," I reminded her.

"Well, I will if it's a booze cruise. This is gonna be the most fun ever!"

I excused myself to my room and called my mother in a panic.

I explained to my mother that if I continued along my path of despair, I knew I would end up hurting Dumb Dumb either mentally or, more likely, physically. I also admitted to being a part-time smoker and that I would be forced to take it up more seriously if forced to vacation with Dumb Dumb. My mother told me that life isn't always about pleasing yourself and that sometimes you have to do things for the sole benefit of another human being. I completely agreed with her, but reminded her that that was what blow jobs were for. She said that Dumb Dumb was a twenty-eight-year-old virgin who was looking at this like the vacation of a lifetime and that I needed to have a positive attitude rather than sulk and think nasty thoughts. It was curious to me that my mother could have such wise insights, but when finding a joint in my room years earlier blurted out, "Oh this is just fantastic. So now you're smoking cigarettes?" My mother went on to say how fortunate I was to have been exposed to so much and that I should support people who were less cultured. My mom made it sound like I was a debutante who had just been accepted to the Sorbonne and that Dumb Dumb had been born on the New Jersey Turnpike. I liked this inference and decided to adopt a new attitude.

It's funny how things work. If you pretend to be excited about something you're not looking forward to, eventually you will start to believe it. Within days, I was on an absolute high talking about the adventures we would have on board our cruise ship. I didn't even blink when I heard Dumb Dumb mention that we would be sailing on the Carnival Cruise line. "Sounds great!" I said with my teeth tightly clenched; I was not going to allow myself to say anything negative about the cruise line or that maniac, Kathie Lee Gifford.

I started imagining all the ballrooms there would be for me to model my new Roberto Cavalli shoes in. I had no dress to wear with them, but I hoped to find something at Express. I pictured a wonderfully romantic episode of *The Love Boat*. I would be on the Lido Deck late one starry night in an evening gown looking for the Big Dipper, when a Leonardo DiCaprio look-alike would come up and take me from behind. We would be on the bow and spread our arms out to the sea, and I would yell, "You are the king of the world!"

And who knew what kind of exciting outdoor activities they had? Everyone had told me about all the amazing food on cruises; I couldn't wait to gorge myself on rack of lamb and fresh lobster. Dumb Dumb asked me if I thought they caught the fish right out of the ocean and then served it on board that night. "Probably," I responded. "It seems like the most logical thing to do."

I believed in this cruise and knew it was going to be fun. I daydreamed about all the different love connections that would be made on different floors of our ship. People in and out of cabin doors in the wee hours of the night, walking down the plush red carpets, while upstairs in the Grand Ballroom I would be closing down the dance floor with my new Leo look-alike to a covered rendition of Carly Simon's "Give Me All Night."

Dumb Dumb even agreed to buy a book for the cruise— something she could read while we were lying out in between pool dips. We went to a Barnes & Noble, where I picked up an unauthorized biography of M. C. Hammer, and not wanting to overload her on her first book, I steered Dumb Dumb toward a *Choose Your Own Adventure*.

The cruise was a four-day, three-night voyage that left from Long Beach and returned on New Year's Day. The morning of the cruise we needed to check in at the dock at nine a.m. I had been in such high spirits leading up to the trip that it was no problem for me to get up at seven thirty to be there on time, sporting my amazing new attitude while doing so. I was rethinking my whole approach to this game they called Life. Maybe Dumb Dumb was not so stupid after all. Happiness *is* a choice. I had only just begun preaching my new belief system to Ivory and Lydia, who suddenly and inexplicably stopped speaking to me.

When we got to the dock, we went to Customs and showed our identification. As if loads of Americans were illegally trying to immigrate to Mexico. We checked our bags and got on line with some of our fellow passengers. Judging from the looks of them, it was clear that they were members of a different income bracket from the people I preferred to surround myself with. But since I also wasn't from the income bracket I preferred, I held off on voicing my initial feelings of despair. I was going to give this cruise my best shot. I pointed to a guy standing at the end of the line. "That guy was just totally checking you out," I lied.

"Really?" she asked. "Where?"

"Over there, over there." I pointed again. She saw him.

"He's not even that cute" was her reply. He wasn't that cute, but she was no Miss New Jersey either, so I was surprised at her laissez-faire attitude. I hoped she wasn't thinking about dabbling in my pool of men. I had been at this game awhile and knew my male equivalence. She obviously didn't realize that you needed to stay within realistic boundaries. Dumb Dumb had a few extra pounds on her and, as far as I could tell, wasn't in any hurry to lose them. She wasn't fat, but she wasn't going to be exposing her belly in a half shirt anytime soon without people quickly looking away.

"Well, someone seems to be very picky there, missy," I said.

"I have a good feeling about this cruise," she told me. "I just know I'm going to meet someone."

I knew there was a better chance of me giving birth to a penguin than Dumb Dumb meeting her soul mate aboard this cruise ship, but my new loving heart prevailed. My main focus was going to be getting her penetrated, or at least fondled. My second objective would be getting myself penetrated. My mother had convinced me that I was a giver, and though I had my doubts, I took on my new role with pride.

As we walked the plank to board the vessel, that pride made a quick exit and I started to get the feeling you get right after a bad batch of sushi: nausea, not unlike sea sickness, but this was more of a visceral disgust. This boat was a fucking mess. The feculent aroma coming from what I could only conjecture was the carpet was a smell I had experienced once before when waking up in a bar. The carpets had some horrible psychedelic design that appeared to be silk-screened on top in a fruitless attempt to cover the wide assortment of stains.

Some of the crew members were wearing blue shirts with the Carnival logo on them and some crew members were just wearing their own clothing with a name tag and a Carnival Cruise pin. Some had their shirts tucked in, some didn't. The crew looked completely disinterested, almost mentally off somehow, and there were framed photographs on the wall of more disinterested employees, all of which were crooked. Most of the crew members didn't even look eighteen. I began to have serious concerns about the kind of operation they were running.

Dumb Dumb grabbed my arm and said, "Let's just go to our room, we have a *suite*." I couldn't respond because I was still in a state of shock, overwhelmed by a disgust that can only be associated with deep disappointment or a keen sense of smell.

We went to our cabin, which meant hiking up four flights of stairs and down a hallway that was barely wide enough to fit one person—who was walking sideways. Where was this piece of shit boat when they were filming *The Love Boat*? We opened our door to find a pair of bunk beds and a porthole with glass so thick it was impossible to decipher whether the blue on the other side was the ocean or the sky.

"Is that our ocean view?" I asked Dumb Dumb as I tripped over the threshold. Apparently, we were moving.

"Oh, my gosh," she said. "This is pretty bad." She started to laugh. I did not.

"I can't stay here," I said. "I can't do it."

"It's not that bad," she said. "We can't leave. The ship has already left the dock."

"We'll have to swim to shore," I told her.

"Stop it! It'll be like a great big adventure!" she said.

I needed to find Captain Stubing right away—and Isaac and the doc. Where was that coked-up whore, Julie? Those were my peeps. I wanted to stay in their big, grand bedrooms with king-size beds and maid service.

After I regained my composure, I realized it was time to formulate a plan. Step one was to start drinking immediately. I was always more logical when I drank. Step two was to devise a means of escape.

We dropped our bags and I went to the bathroom to check in with myself. The bathroom was about four feet by four feet with a toilet that you had to step over to get into the shower. I stared intently at this absurd setup, trying to figure out where to put my legs while peeing as there were only about two inches between the front of the toilet and the bathroom wall. I opted to put my feet in the shower as I sat sideways on the toilet seat. I called Dumb Dumb in so she could witness what this cruise was really about.

"Oh, my gosh! Oh, my gosh! How are we supposed to go to the bathroom?" she asked.

"Is this your fucking *suite*? This is what I paid nine hundred dollars for?"

"I am so sorry. I'll pay for my end. You don't have to pay for me," she said.

"Good. I'd like it in cash," I told her.

We left our "suite" to go check out the ship and get some drinks in us. Dumb Dumb picked up an activities pamphlet, which informed us that the casino would open as soon as we left the California border. Things were looking up. Gambling was a favorite pastime of mine, and combined with being on water, memories of my favorite movie, *Porky's,* flooded into my brain. We went to exchange our money for gambling chips and waited on line behind a woman who was wearing two fanny packs around her waist and missing a front tooth.

After that, we made our way up to the Lido Deck, where we checked out the pool situation and got some drinks at the bar. There was a man sitting at the bar with hair down to his waist and wearing cutoff black jeans. The problem with his hair was that the better part of his head was bald, and the long stringy hair that remained was coming from behind his ears.

I went up to the only bald man with split ends I had ever seen and asked him how to get a drink around here.

"I'll get it for you," he replied.

"Do you work here?" I asked.

"Sometimes," was his response.

Dumb Dumb grimaced, but I pressed on. "I'll take a Ketel One with anything. Two of them."

"Where's the pool?" I asked our bartender. He pointed behind us toward a circular tank that looked like something out of Sea World, except it had no water and was covered with a decorative red, white, and blue tarp. "Is that it?" I asked him.

"That's one of 'em. There's about four more all over, but it's off season so they're all closed up."

"Off season?" asked Dumb Dumb.

"Yes ma'am. November to February," he said as he handed us our drinks in plastic Dixie cups.

"Now do you want to swim to shore?" I asked Dumb Dumb.

We thanked Split Ends for our drinks before I realized they were made out of cheap vodka and Kool-Aid, which Dumb Dumb of course loved, because it reminded her of nursery school.

There was no one else on the Lido Deck, so we made our way down a couple of decks. When I spotted my third mullet, I told Dumb Dumb that we should just go back to our rooms and sleep.

"We should at least lie out," she said.

"It's not even sixty degrees out," I told her.

"That's when you get the best color," she told me.

We got our bathing suits and a dinner menu and went back up to the Lido Deck. Split Ends was still there. I asked him for a real vodka in a real glass but he told me they served only plastic except at dinner. He ignored my comment about the real vodka.

"When is dinner?" Dumb Dumb asked.

"You can eat at seven or at nine in the formal dining room," he said.

"Is the formal dining room formal?" I asked.

"Hell, yeah," he said. "No shorts, no sneakers, no half shirts."

"No problem," I said.

It was too windy to get into our bathing suits so we just sat on our plastic chaise longues in front of the tarped-up pool/tank and stared at the sky. I thought about taking the tarp off and diving in headfirst; I'm sure I wouldn't have been the first. I tried calling 911, but my cell phone wasn't getting any reception. This was a disaster. My positive attitude had long since joined the witness protection program, but I tried to stay calm.

Dumb Dumb asked me which dinner seating I wanted to go to and I told her the seven o'clock one, because I hoped by nine to be unconscious. Apparently the casino wouldn't open until the next day (big surprise), so we just continued drinking. We passed out on our chairs or, as I like to say, put ourselves down for a nap, sometime after one and woke up to find ourselves surrounded by seagulls feeding on the peanuts left on the bar. Just when I thought things couldn't get any worse, someone announced over the loudspeaker that a shuffleboard contest was starting on the Lido Deck in five minutes. It was time to move on.

We flipped through the boat's guide of idiotic activities and decided to play bingo in the Carnival Room at five. We sat next to a couple who told us they were getting married on the boat. This news sent Dumb Dumb into a tizzy.

"Married! That is sooo romantic. Where did you guys meet? How did you propose?" I wanted to remind Dumb Dumb that there was nothing romantic about getting married on a Carnival cruise *or* having matching ZZ Top shirts, but I didn't want to hurt their feelings.

This cruise was also going to be their honeymoon because the woman couldn't get more than a week off from the power plant where she worked. That was the last thing I heard before I yelled, "Bingo!"

"Shut up! Shut up! You got it?!" yelled the woman. The master of ceremonies pointed me out in the crowd and I stood up as everyone applauded.

"Just kidding," I said and walked out.

I was getting very drunk and needed fresh air. Dumb Dumb followed me, but I told her I needed to be alone. "Are you going to jump?" she asked.

"No, I'm not going to jump, but I need to eat soon. I'm wasted."

"Well, stop drinking," she told me.

"That's not really an option."

It was a quarter to seven as we walked outside to the Yellow Deck and walked a lap. Dumb Dumb suggested we run back to the room to get ready. "Get ready for *what?*" I asked her.

We headed to our assigned table in the dining room and saw three women in their midforties sitting there. "Great. Look at our table," I told her.

We sat down with the ladies at our round table, leaving us with five empty seats. "Hello, ladies," Dumb Dumb said and started the introductions. They were very sweet, prim and proper ladies who were clearly from some town with no television or magazines. "We're from Nebraska," one of the women said, which happened to be one of the states I suspected. The only surprise was that anyone would actually *fly in* for this cruise. They giggled devilishly as they told us they were on a "girls only" trip away from their husbands. I could tell the raciest things these women had ever been involved in was a co-ed game of Connect Four.

After about a minute of small talk, the skinny, dark-haired woman with the palest skin I'd ever seen asked, "Are you Christians?"

"Yes, I am Christian," said Dumb Dumb.

"Oh, how lovely," they said. "So nice to meet you." The women immediately warmed.

"No, you're not a Christian," I told Dumb Dumb. "You're Presbyterian. That's very different." This was so typical of Dumb Dumb. She didn't know anything about herself.

"Well, whatever," Dumb Dumb said. "I believe in Jesus Christ."

This is exactly why I didn't want to go on vacation with her. She had no loyalty. She was as bad as my sister Sloane. I didn't want to be the only nonbeliever at the table. Luckily, I was drunk enough to defend myself.

"I'm a Jew," I told them and ordered a double Ketel One and cranberry. Certainly the "formal" dining room served real vodka, I thought.

"That's nice," one of the women replied.

And just like that, as if I hadn't said anything at all, the ladies sprang into a conversation about the sinful nature the Jews possessed when killing their Lord Jesus. I didn't know if I was hearing this right because I had become so intoxicated, but I couldn't believe that anyone would talk about religion while on vacation. How could Miss Nebraska think this was a proper environment to discuss something so controversial? One woman went on to say that if she had her way, not only would President Bush serve a second four-year term, but she hoped they would overturn *Roe v. Wade*. This woman was obviously a menace to society and needed to be stopped.

"Excuse me," I interrupted, "I have a question. Is it okay to drink while you're pregnant...? You're planning on giving the baby up for adoption?" This time Dumb Dumb didn't follow me outside.

There were four Mexican guys hanging around on the Lido Deck. I will refer to them as "cholos" only because one of them was wearing a hat that said, "CHOLO."

"What's up, homeys?" I asked as I slid down in a chaise longue next to them. They were smoking pot out of something that looked like a cigar. "Is that a spliff?" I asked.

"Yes, *mija*, would you like to take a puff?" I had learned my lesson the hard way about laced marijuana and was too drunk to smoke marijuana that wasn't laced.

"No thanks, homey. You guys heading back to Mexico?"

One of the guys came over. "My name is Rico," he said. He wore white volleyball socks up to his knees with cutoff tan Dickies and a thick black belt. A white wife-beater tank top completed his outfit. His head was shaved, but he had a bushy mustache.

As Rico sat down next to me, I leaned over and violently threw up. His three friends backed away in disgust. I felt embarrassed but I couldn't stop heaving. I vaguely remember the three guys saying something about leaving, but Rico opted to stay by my side and hold my hair.

He finally moved me to where I could throw up over the balcony, and I spent the next four hours doing just that. I couldn't move an inch and he understood completely. At one point he took a rubber band out of his pocket and put my hair in a ponytail. This guy was turning out to be very dependable. Without him, there was a good chance I would've fallen overboard. He looked through my pockets to find my key, and around midnight, he said it was time for him to take me to my cabin.

"I'll sleep here, just leave me alone," I cried.

"No, *mija*, you cannot sleep here. You will freeze like a turkey."

It was pretty cold, but I doubt I would have frozen, and I wished he hadn't brought up Thanksgiving.

After another hour I agreed to let him carry me back to my cabin, which was not an easy route to negotiate considering the narrowness of the hallways. People glared at us as he strode inside with me in his arms like a scene out of *The English Patient* and asked if everything was okay. I tried to answer them but could only slur.

As he opened the door to our room, Dumb Dumb flew to her feet in her *Shrek* pajamas and screamed, "Oh, my God, are you okay?" Then, "Who the fuck are you?"

"Calm down, *mija,* I am just delivering your friend," Rico said.

"Get out," she screamed. "Heeeeeelp!"

"Yo, yo, yo, chill, lady, chill," he said and then turned around to leave as she picked up a shoe and hurled it in his direction.

"Thanks," I slurred as I heard the door shut. I climbed into the lower bunk bed. "Shut up, he took care of me," I told Dumb Dumb as I passed out.

When I woke up the next morning, feeling five pounds lighter, I informed Dumb Dumb that we needed to get off the ship at Ensenada and pay some Mexicans to drive us to Los Angeles. "I *cannot* spend New Year's Eve on this boat."

"No way, that's crazy. We could get raped," she said.

"Well, at least we'd have a good New Year's!" I yelled. Rape didn't sound as bad as spending another day on this cruise. "Think about it," I said. "I know they have those parasailing rides on the beaches in Mexico; maybe we could parasail back." Then I rolled over and went back to sleep.

"You can gamble now. We're in Mexico," Dumb Dumb said when she woke me up two hours later.

Immediately, I felt better. Since I would need a cheeseburger and a couple of hours to recover before my next cocktail, we headed to the cafeteria for lunch. I explained to her over the world's most disgusting cheeseburger that Rico had taken good care of me last night and that she shouldn't judge people based on their socks.

"I was scared. I didn't know where you were, and my father told me not to leave the cabin after dark," she said. It was no surprise to me that she had called her father. She called him several times a day in New Jersey to ask him things like whether it was going to rain in California and if it was okay to eat at Subway, the sandwich chain. My favorite piece of advice he had given her was to never use tampons and only wear maxipads because, "There's a killer out there, and its name is toxic shock syndrome." I wanted to tell her father that I was living proof that a tampon could survive inside of a woman for up to three days before any real symptoms flared up, but I was becoming more adept at picking my battles.

I asked Dumb Dumb if she thought any more about my idea for getting back to Los Angeles.

"My father said no way, it would be way too dangerous," she told me.

I thought about going it alone, but I couldn't leave her here on this ship by herself. Still, I couldn't believe this boat was where I was meant to wreak havoc on New Year's Eve.

"Fine," I said. "Let's go gamble. I'll teach you how to play blackjack."

I gambled for close to eight hours straight with Dumb Dumb standing guard. I was up four hundred dollars and was feeling great. She was too nervous to waste any of her own money, so finally I gave her one hundred dollars in chips and she played with that. She appeared to be winning, but she always bet the minimum amount, which was good because it meant she was occupied for a longer period of time.

I would have been happy gambling into the wee hours of the morning if necessary and asked our dealer how late he was open. "For the next thirty hours," he said, "until we get back to California." That's when the Scott Wolf look-alike walked past our table. I hadn't had anything to drink yet, and his presence alone was reason enough to celebrate. He wasn't as cute as Scott Wolf, but neither was anyone else on this cruise. He had lighter hair and a rather stocky physique for someone not much taller than five-five. Dumb Dumb elbowed me. We both knew he was by far the best-looking guy on this boat, and his smooth, soft skin reminded me of myself a couple of months earlier.

"Don't even think about it," I said through a tight smile. "You can have Rico."

I looked over at the boy who was saving my New Year's and said, "Excuse me, would you mind coming over here a minute?"

"Sure," he said and walked over to us.

"Is your name Kevin?" I asked him. This was my new favorite pickup line.

"No," he said.

"Really? Do I look familiar to you?"

"A little bit," he told me. That meant he was interested.

"Well this is Dumb Dumb and I'm Single," I told him.

"Shut up, that is *not* my name," she said.

He was laughing now and I knew I would have sex with him. "Do you have any friends with you?" I asked.

"Sure," he said. "A bunch of us will be at Club Paradise on the Upper Deck in about an hour. Would you like to join us?" I thought about reminding him that this was a cruise ship and if we did show up at Club Paradise it didn't necessarily mean we were joining *him*, but I kept my mouth shut.

"We'll meet you there," I said. He was very cute and I was elated. It turned out that, after all, showers would be necessary. "Let's go get ready," I told Dumb Dumb.

She was more excited than a chimpanzee holding a banana. "Oh, my gosh! This is amazing! Do you think his friends will be cute too? What should I wear? I'm so excited. I hope there's dancing."

I hoped there wasn't dancing, but I wasn't going to let that spoil my only chance of a hookup on New Year's. This would be my third New Year's in a row that I was single, and I wasn't going to let it go by without hooking up. If a fourth New Year's went by without any action I would be in an official slump.

We took showers with our flip-flops on in an effort to avoid direct contact with the carpet, and while we dressed, I drank three more plastic cups filled with vodka and switched to orange juice for some vitamin C. Having missed dinner on purpose in order to avoid another confrontation with John Ashcroft's wife, I downed a couple of PowerBars to ensure enough stamina on the dance floor. I looked hot and, most of all, skinny. I love the day after throwing up. I felt like a feather.

We went up to Club Paradise, which is an interesting name for anything on a ship that should have been sunk by a torpedo years earlier. I spotted my B-version of Scott Wolf surrounded by a couple of other corpulent figures. They all had the same clean-cut college boy look going on, and they all seemed like they were in their early twenties. I was twenty-six at the time and figured I had to take what I could get at this point on my trip. It's not that my guy wasn't cute, but if we had been on land, his having a full set of teeth wouldn't have been an added bonus.

As usual, Dumb Dumb was clinging to me, so I made one of his friends ask her to dance. This gave me an opportunity to get my man alone. Plus, I don't like to make my moves in front of an audience.

His name was Les, which sounded like a child molester's name, but again I knew this was probably God testing me, and I had to take what was thrown my way. As soon as I saw Dumb Dumb start relaxing with her guy, I leaned in and asked Les if he had his own cabin.

"No, I'm sharing one," he said. "But my roommate is on the dance floor."

"Well, do you have bunk beds?" I asked him.

"Yeah, we do," he smiled in a cute, embarrassed way.

"You want to go back to your cabin and fool around?" I asked him.

"Absofuckinglutely," was his answer. I thought that was a pretty bold response for someone of such little stature. I was starting to like this guy more and more. I loved a man/boy with confidence.

I told Dumb Dumb that Les wanted to show me his cabin and that I'd be back in an hour. She wasn't happy about it, so I gave her some food for thought. I explained that this cruise was going to be like a coming-out party for her and if she showed signs of maturing out of adolescence and into the beginning stages of adulthood, who knew how many more vacations together were in the cards for us. When that didn't seem to work, I promised her a year's subscription to *Tiger Beat*.

I was pretty buzzed from having almost nothing in my stomach and I needed some cardio. That's why when the door to Les's cabin hadn't even closed all the way and he had already thrown me onto the lower bunk bed, I showed no signs of a struggle. In fact, I was turned on by how forceful he was and could not imagine his penis being any smaller than a standard-size lint brush. I was auditioning him for my New Year's Eve sex partner, and so far it looked like he was definitely getting a callback.

Boy, did I underestimate Les. Not only was his penis larger than average, he had the stamina of the Iraqi ground forces. He had the exact same physique as Serena Williams. Things were happening that even I couldn't keep up with. Before I knew it, not only were my clothes off, but somehow I was on the top bunk. Les launched into a vault across the room to the porthole, where he grabbed a condom and then triple salchowed back up to me. This guy belonged in the Olympics—and not the ones I would have qualified for. All of a sudden, he was on top of me. Just before we started having sex, he flipped me around and I was on all fours. I had never been manhandled like this before and was really enjoying myself. This cruise was turning out to be an episode of *The Love Boat*, after all; I would have to check tomorrow about availability for next year.

That's when Les hit me. Not a slap or a caress, just an open-handed full throttle strike against my right ass cheek. It was with such force that not only did I cough, I almost flew off the bed. In the couple of seconds it took me to remember his name, he hit me three more times, alternating ass cheeks.

"Hey! You! Stop that!" I managed to yell out.

"What's the matter?" he stopped to ask.

"Did you just hit me?" I turned to look at him so he wasn't staring at the back of my head.

"You don't like that?" he asked me in a soft voice. Now he was back to his original self.

"Well, I don't know, I guess...wasn't I doing good?" was the nonsense that left my mouth in the form of a question. Spanking was usually something you discuss beforehand. I felt a little violated and thought that after we were done I was going to be forced to make him a sandwich or something.

"You seem like you like it," he said breathing heavily. The truth was that I did kind of like it, but at the same time, it seemed so violent that I felt as if I should object. I was in a tailspin of confusion I hadn't experienced since the first time I heard George W. Bush speak. It wasn't that I didn't like confrontation. I did, but I had never had a disagreement during the act of sex before and I hadn't known Les long enough to have our first fight. I thought about hitting him back, but that seemed too manufactured. It was usually me calling the shots in bed, and I didn't know how to react to someone else taking the wheel. Especially when we were technically the same size.

"It's okay, I guess," I told him. And so it continued, for the next fifteen minutes until he climaxed, which, coincidentally, also bordered on bearlike behavior.

"How old are you?" I asked him after we were done. I

was lying on the top bunk and he had moved to the bottom. I was lonely and felt like making small talk. I had never been left so quickly after sex before, though I had done it many times to others. Now that the shoe was on the other foot, I began to realize what abandonment was all about.

"I'll be nineteen on January first," he told me.

"I really need to get back to my friend," I told him as I lunged off the top bunk, naked, with one hand covering my vagina and the other covering my right boob. My left boob was out for the taking, but in an effort to avoid it getting hit, I turned and quickly put on my clothes.

In my drunken stupor I was still trying to figure out how I could have ended up in bed with an almost minor. This wasn't good at all. I had never slept with someone even a year younger than me and immediately felt like R. Kelly. How did a boy that young learn how to spank women? I feared that maybe he was lying about his age and wasn't even legal; images of the water police taking me off the ship in handcuffs and ankle weights swam through my mind.

The next night was New Year's Eve, and we decided to see a show called *Swing, Swing, Swing* since my gambling streak was over and I was now down two hundred dollars. As we were being seated, I saw Rico a couple of rows behind us. "Hey, Rico," I yelled, *"cómo te llamas?"* He looked at me and my roommate and then made a gesture that was similar to the middle finger, but the Spanish version that tells someone you're not interested in speaking with them.

"You really pissed that guy off, now he won't even talk to us," I told Dumb Dumb. "Thanks for taking care of me!" I screamed out, and this time he made a gesture I hadn't seen before. I didn't understand why he was pissed at me. I never threw a shoe at him.

As the mangy curtains separated to start the show, the first person out on stage was a bare-chested male wearing green tights with a long run down one leg and a fake wreath on his head. He sprang onto the floor with a combination of two back handsprings followed by a half pike into a somersault. I would have recognized those moves at sea or on land. It was official: I had now hit my all-time low at the tender age of twenty-six. Not only did I sleep with an eighteen-year-old who hit me, but he was the lead in an abysmal cruise dance show called, *Swing, Swing, Swing.*

Maybe a real boyfriend wasn't the worst thing that could happen to a girl.

I WAS ON the Discovery Channel's website trying to get my hands on a monkey when my cell phone rang. Nathan called to ask me if I would be his beard at his high school reunion.

Somehow, Nathan still considers himself a closet homosexual even though anyone who has ever spent a late night at his apartment knows otherwise. You didn't have to clear a thousand on your SATs to figure out that when you were abruptly getting kicked out of his apartment at one a.m., and a tall beefy Latino passed you on his way in, that Nathan had ordered takeout from We Deliver Cock.

All Nathan's classmates from high school and college, along with his parents, were still in the dark about his homosexuality. His parents had no idea that when they sent him to a child psychiatrist at the age of fifteen, he began a romantic relationship with his shrink that lasted for well over ten years. "Romance" isn't the word I would use to describe your psychiatrist giving you head, but Nathan insisted that the relationship was a two-way street and they had strong romantic feelings for each other. This was obviously the Jews' retaliation for not having access to the

Catholic church and their pedophiles. Being as resourceful as we are, we developed our own system of child molestation and then added another layer by paying our attacker.

After receiving this information from Nathan, I was thoroughly disappointed that none of my therapists had ever tried to go down on me. Nathan admitted this relationship to me only after we had been friends for many years, and when he did, it was primarily to convince me to accompany him on his family vacation and pose as his girlfriend.

"Will the psychiatrist be there?" I asked.

"No."

"Then why would I want to go?"

"Because my parents want to meet you. I talk about you all the time, and this way they'll think I'm closer to getting married."

"But you're not getting married. Certainly not to me," I told him. In fact, we'd discussed marriage on several occasions just because we seemed to get along so well, but after thinking long and hard, I realized it was not in my best interest to waste my first marriage on a gay man.

But Nathan convinced me to come along and I ended up going on many more family vacations with him after that. There was the trip to Telluride, ten days in Fiji, and a couple of weekends at his family's house in Big Bear. It was turning out to be a swell deception and I was getting a lot of frequent flyer miles in return. His family was fun, and I liked his overbearing Jewish mother who wanted to know everything about me, from my favorite sexual position to my rising sign. She would sit and play with my hair and stare at me like I was Goldilocks, saying over and over again how she couldn't believe I was Jewish. My mother is the antithesis of a typical Jewish mother; she is very soft-spoken and takes more naps than a cat. As a result, I've always longed for someone to really annoy the shit out of me.

Normally I would say yes to a high school reunion, but I was still pissed about my sister's wedding. Thanks to Nathan's catastrophic visit to my parents' summer home, I was banned from bringing anyone home again.

So when Nathan asked me to go to his high school reunion that wasn't really a reunion, more like an annual summer cocktail party for all the alumni who had attended his prep school, I refused.

"Come on, pleeeease, it will be so much fun. It's at the Bel-Air Bay Club, there's an open bar, and there will be hot men." These were all valid arguments, but I wasn't giving in. I was seriously considering cutting him off for good.

"I'm not even sure I ever want to see you again," I told him.

"Don't say that!" he hissed. "It wasn't that bad, you're totally overreacting. I even got a thank-you card from your sister. She *loved* me."

I felt unsure about believing him, but it was so typical of my sister to help me not make a point.

"A thank-you card?" I asked. "Thank you for *what*? Ruining her wedding? How would she even get your address?"

"It was probably on the bottle of Valium I gave her," he replied. "She was a real wreck before she went down the aisle. I only gave her a half because she said she'd never done any before, but after the ceremony she wanted more, so I gave her the bottle."

Now I was fuming. How could I have missed the opportunity to pop pills with my sister who was purer than a Quaker? I was torn between being angry at Nathan and being proud of my sister for finally loosening up her sphincter. This was a girl who, when I was ten years old, used to wake me up after she got home from a party and whisper, "Chelsea, wake up. They had marijuana at the party and I didn't smoke any."

I'd roll over, crack my eyes open, and say, "Why *not*?"

"Nathan, you are ridiculous, you have no respect for anyone. How many times have I been to your parents' house or on vacation and not only behaved myself but quoted actual verses from the Torah?"

"What if I pay you?" he asked.

I had always dreamed of being a professional escort but never thought that there was any real money in it. "How much?" I asked.

"Two hundred dollars," he offered.

I guffawed loudly and then pretended to choke. "Homo you don't!" I said. "That's not enough money to pretend I like you again."

"Please, please, just come with me, it will be fun, we can both meet people."

We had done this type of thing before, on numerous occasions. I would hit on a guy whom Nathan liked, and if he didn't respond to me, Nathan would move in. This way no one ever found out that Nathan was indeed a flaming homosexual, unless Nathan ended up sleeping with him, in which case he definitely knew. The problem with this approach was that Nathan was obsessed with huge lumberjack-type men, preferably with a pickup truck, so if the guy I came on to wasn't gay, I'd usually end up getting stalked and forced to make a quick getaway out the back entrance of some seedy bar.

"I'm not picking up guys for you," I said. "Not for two hundred dollars."

"These guys are all from my prep school, there won't be any dumb ones, I prooooomise," he said.

"*You're* dumb and you're going to be there," I reminded him.

"There's my girl. You'll do it?"

"Not for two hundred," I told him. "I'll need some other incentive."

"I'll buy you a dress, from wherever you want. You get it and I'll reimburse you—no more than two hundred and fifty dollars."

"That sounds reasonable," I said in my best impression of a litigator.

I ended up spending less on the dress than the two fifty allotted me by my gay pimp because Barneys was having a 75 percent off sale, so I also bought a head scarf in case it became windy. It was actually a neck scarf, but I had seen J. Lo wrap her head with one and tie it at the nape of her neck, which split the silk into two different sections of flowing magic. The shade of my dress was a hot pink more accurately described as "summer whore" and the head scarf was cream with rings of citrus, lavender, and summer whore as well. I had never worn a head scarf publicly before and was looking forward to finally commanding the respect I deserved.

Nathan picked me up in a town car outside my apartment. He did this when he wanted to impress. He claimed he was just being responsible because we would be drinking, but considering he had been convicted of three separate DUIs, I knew better.

"Look at you!" he squealed as I made my way to the car. "Three words: beau-teee-ful!"

"Thank you," I replied with the cool air of an aristocrat. I wasn't giving in to him that easily; he was going to have to work for my forgiveness.

The Bel-Air Bay Club is located north of Malibu and overlooks the Pacific Ocean. Throughout the course of our ride, when I wasn't staring out the window I had rolled down to aid my scarf in a current of strong wind, I was reminding Nathan of how lucky he was to have a friend like me.

"You better drop this shit when we get to the party. I said I was sorry *and* sent a letter apologizing to your parents."

"Well, I hope you did. I am not allowed to ever bring anyone back there again!"

"Listen, I'm sorry and I know I drank too much, but let's focus on tonight," he said. "You could meet your future husband here. There are a lot of rich and successful young men who went to this school."

"I'm not that shallow, asshole. I don't need money," I said. "It's way more important for them to be good-looking."

We finally arrived at the front door of the club and the

car slowed. "You are my girlfriend unless I tell you otherwise," he reminded me as our driver opened our door.

We checked in at the front and they gave us name tags. I wasn't about to ruin my ensemble with such a cheesy name tag, not to mention the blatant clash of color; the Magic Marker the woman was writing names with was fire engine red. I was already going out on a limb with the head scarf and didn't want anyone to think I was trying to one-up Sarah Jessica Parker.

I told the woman I'd put mine on my purse, and she said she'd prefer if I wore it on my dress. Then I told her I wasn't part of the alumni and that no one would be recognizing me anyway.

"That's not the point, dear. It's just better if everyone's names are displayed so that the lines of communication have already opened."

I thought maybe she was trying to be funny but then realized this was impossible to do without a sense of humor.

"What's your name, dear?" she said.

"Beulah. My name is Beulah," I told her.

Her eyes darted from mine to Nathan's, but he backed me up with a quick nod in her direction.

"How is that spelled?" she asked.

"Just as it sounds, B-e-u-l-a-h," I said. Then she ripped off the adhesive and stuck it right above my right breastplate. "I love your head ornament," she said with a closed smile.

"I love your personality!" I said with wide eyes and an open smile. I had used this look before when a bank teller at Wells Fargo had threatened to put a ten-day hold on a check from my father because my average balance was $3.56.

Nathan grabbed me by the arm and pulled me toward the patio. There were various food stations all around and two bars positioned at either end.

"I'll get us drinks, you find somewhere to sit," I told him. I went to the bar and ordered two Ketel One and sodas.

"Fourteen dollars, please," the bartender said.

"This isn't an open bar?" I asked.

"Only for well drinks," he told me. "The well vodka is Gordon's."

"Who's Gordon?" I asked him.

He half smiled at me, shrugging only one of his shoulders.

"Hold on," I said and ran over to Nathan. "Give me money, it's not an open bar. This party is starting out very badly, Nathan. Not so good, so far!" I intimated that an unhappy Chelsea would lead to unhappy times. He got the message.

After I paid for our drinks, I came back to find Nathan being harassed by a middle-aged white woman wearing a strapless cotton-poly blend that pushed her breasts out like a shelf. Her blond hair was three shades too light and she was holding what I presumed could only be a chardonnay. Women like this love chardonnay, especially while it's still light out. She seemed very taken with Nathan, as many women were; he has a way of making women feel beautiful and sexy, which is why my friends and I liked him so much in the first place.

She kept moving closer to him and I didn't want to steal her moment, so I discreetly took a seat at the table behind where they were standing and observed. Five minutes later, she noticed me and introduced herself. "I'm Lynn," she said, extending her free hand.

"Beulah, how are you?" Nathan said.

"Oh, I'm sorry, are you two..." she pointed back and forth between us.

"Oh no, no, no, he's just my swim instructor, we're very close, but not like that." I winked at her.

Nathan turned his head in order to avoid eye contact with me and with her.

"Are you a professional swimmer?" she asked.

"Synchronized swimming, actually. I'm the only professional synchronizer who can compete without a nose plug," I told her.

"Is that right?" she asked excitedly. "How are you able to do that?"

"It's not easy," I told her. "I've trained myself to hold my breath underwater as well as above water for close to six minutes at a time. Each competition is five minutes." I, of course, didn't have the faintest idea if this was true, but five minutes sounded like a reasonable time to be able to hold your breath. Why anyone needed to hold her breath above water was beyond me, but when I make things up, I rarely have a filter.

She had a confused look on her face and opened her mouth to say something when I jumped in.

"There's a good chance I'll be competing in Athens in 2004."

Nathan coughed loudly and sat down, "Actually—"

I interrupted. "He's so superstitious, he doesn't like me

to talk about the Olympics before the trials, he thinks I'll jinx myself," I said dismissively. "I keep telling him God gave me a talent and there's nothing to jinx about that."

"Amen!" she said.

"Hallelujah!" I responded.

She turned to Nathan and put her hand on his arm. "A swim coach. You must be in fantastic shape!" Nathan smiled sheepishly as I got up to excuse myself.

"I'm going to see if I can't find a fish in this big swimming pool. You kids get to know each other." Nathan averted his eyes and looked down at his hands in his lap. I winked at the woman and mouthed, "He's single!"

I wandered over into another room dominated by a massive chandelier. The club was huge and extravagant, with four separate patios. I love places that are spread out like that; this way once you embarrass yourself in one area, another forum is just a hop, skip, and jump away.

This being an all-boys school, there were guaranteed to be dozens of men to harass. I sauntered over to the sushi bar, filled my plate, and went to sit by a window all by my lonesome. I put on a sad, wounded, dovelike expression to let any potential male suitors know I was available and, more important, vulnerable.

After a good ten minutes of no one approaching me, I saw a hottie walk by me in a beautiful Ted Baker shirt. I knew Ted Baker shirts like the back of my hand, and anyone who wears one deserves to be complimented.

"Excuse me," I said as he glanced around, trying to see where the voice was coming from, "I absolutely love your shirt."

"Thank you," he said, finally noticing me. He smiled. "That's sweet."

"Is it Ted Baker?" I asked.

"Yes, yes it is." He was pleased.

"I used to work for him in London." I wasn't planning on lying, but I needed to keep him here long enough to get my rhythm going.

He sat down next to me and we talked for a couple of minutes about what a brilliant designer Ted was, and then he said, "By the way, I'm David, and you are...Beulah? Is that how you pronounce it?" I couldn't let him think that was my name.

"Oh, no, the lady at the front was a little intense. I was just messing with her. I'm Chelsea."

"That's funny," David said. "Beulah's gotta be one of the ugliest names I've ever heard."

David told me he was a real estate attorney and had just moved back from Atlanta to be close to his family. He didn't know that many people and came here to try and reconnect with some friends from high school. Most of his friends were married and he had just ended a two-year relationship with someone because he hated her family and didn't want to expose his future offspring to them.

"I like your scarf," he said. "Not a lot of people can get away with that look."

I got the feeling he meant that *no one* could get away with the look, and I started laughing. "Point taken," I said and took off my scarf. He quickly wrapped it around his own head. "You're right," I said and pulled it off his head.

This could definitely turn into a relationship. I knew

because I didn't want to sleep with him right away, and I've felt that way only a couple of times. He was solid, good-natured, and most of all he was sarcastic.

He had just asked me who I was there with when I saw Nathan out of the corner of my eye.

"Beulah! There you are! Where have you been, my little bean dip? I hope not flirting with other men," he said as he lowered his lips to mine and kissed me on the mouth. He looked at David. "Oh, hey, I know you, right?" he asked.

"Yes, David Stevenson. I'm sorry, what is your name again?"

"Nathan," said Nathan with a venomous look on his face. "I think you were a year or two older."

"Yes, I think you're right," said David. "So how are you doing?"

"So you met my wife?" Nathan said to my horror.

I started to object, but Nathan jumped in, saying, "It's hard for her since she got out of rehab...I mean to be around other drinkers, you understand." He picked up my drink and sniffed it. "Goddamn it, Beulah! No drinking!" he reprimanded, pointing his finger in my face. Then he shook his head, took me by the elbow, and said, "Let's run along now, dear, shall we?" I couldn't even look at David. There was no point in explaining myself out of that one, so I just turned and walked away, as if everything Nathan said had been true.

"Why are you being such a queen?" I asked him. "He was adorable and he was straight."

"He's an asshole. I know him. You don't want anything to do with him. And he used to think I was gay."

"You *are* gay, assfucker!"

"Shhh," he whispered. "That crazy lady was practically raping me thanks to you, and she works for the school so I couldn't tell her I was gay."

"Oh, I'm so sick of this shit with you. No one cares if you're gay or not already! I need to have a good time too. This is not all about you!" I yelled as we argued in a corner of the patio like an old married couple. Then I left him and walked over to the first table I saw with an available seat.

"Hello," I said to the older black couple who were already sitting there. "Do you mind if I join you?"

"Oh, absolutely, what we need is some young blood around here to liven things up," the woman said with a big warm smile. I liked her instantly.

I used to think I was a black person in a past life because I looooove black people. It's the way they express themselves that draws me to them. White people, for the most part, are too conservative with their emotions and not nearly as effusive as black people when they get excited. If you've ever watched a game show where a white person wins and then, later, a black person wins, you've seen the difference. Black people don't stop and think before they jump up and down in celebration. They are so much more spontaneous and festive, and I've always felt that without that kind of energy, what would be the point of anything.

"Are you and yours having a little tête-à-tête?" the woman asked me, motioning in Nathan's direction. Apparently they had seen our little spat.

"Yes," I said. "He'll be okay, he's just having a little episode. I'm Beulah."

"Well, that's just beautiful. Is it a family name?" she asked me.

"Yes," I said. Technically, it wasn't a lie. Beulah had to be *someone's* family name. The only Beulah I knew of was Beulah Balbricker, the crazy gym teacher in the movie *Porky's* who was a complete mess.

Their names were Valerie and Larry William. I loved the way Valerie spoke. Everything she said rolled off her tongue in a soft mellifluous melody. It had a soothing southern sound to it, and she was one of those people who just kept smiling and whose skin was as smooth as a Milk Dud.

They told me their son had gone to this school, and he was now on the road playing professional basketball, so they had come in his honor. Couples who have been together for so long intrigue me. I am genuinely curious to know what was so different thirty years ago that you actually had a desire to wake up next to the same guy every morning for the rest of your life. Watching Larry rub Valerie's hand, I wanted to be in love like them. But as long as Nathan was around, that wouldn't be happening any time that night.

They were in the middle of telling me about how Larry William proposed to Val when Nathan plopped down in the seat next to me, slammed his drink on the table, and introduced himself. His tie was crooked and he was licking the corner of his mouth, trying to free some hummus. He was clearly drunk, and I had finally had it with his behavior. I didn't know why I was doing him any favors when obviously he had some serious personal issues to deal with.

I decided it was payback time, and it hurt me to have to bring Val and LW into it.

"Hi, honey," I said in the best beaten-wife tone I could muster.

"This is my husband, Nathan," I told Val and LW, "but you wouldn't know it because he refuses to wear his ring."

"That's not true," Nathan said. Nathan meant it wasn't true that we were married, but it came out sounding as if it wasn't true that he actually refuses to wear his ring.

"Junior, that's just plain disrespectful," LW blurted out. I loved that LW had referred to Nathan as Junior. This was turning into a real live sitcom. Nathan was flustered. I jumped in before he could get his bearings.

"It's just so hard. I mean, we've been married for two whole years and he won't even say my name on our outgoing voice mail message." I started to tear up at the thought of this.

"Chelsea!" Nathan blurted.

"Chelsea? Who the hell is Chelsea?" I asked.

"Sorry...Beulah," he corrected himself. LW and Val looked at each other in horror. It was clear to us all that Nathan was having an affair.

"Son, you need to get your head on straight here," cautioned LW. "Now, I don't mean any disrespect, but you have got one hell of a little lady here, and if you don't wake up and smell the cappuccino, somebody else will."

I thought I had died and gone to heaven. Not only was a big black man defending my honor, he had referred to me as little.

Even Nathan couldn't talk back to such an imposing force as LW. LW had James Earl Jones's exact voice and was well over six feet tall, with shoulders you could balance a midget on. Realizing he had no chance against this man and that by resisting or trying to speak he would just come off looking like an asshole, Nathan had to surrender.

"You're right," he said, with his head down where it belonged.

"Now we're getting somewhere," James Earl Jones said.

"It's just so hard because she works all the time," Nathan said, trying to turn the tables, but I wasn't about to let him overtake me.

"What do you do, dear?" asked Val.

"I work with the blind mostly. Some deafs too," I told her.

Nathan spat a little of his drink out.

"See that? He thinks it's funny. He makes fun of them," I said.

"I do not think it's funny. I don't...," he told Val and LW, trying to regain composure. "I just...I just want her... to be home more."

"I *hear* that," LW said.

"Beulah, what exactly do you do with the blind?" Val asked.

"I help them compete in relay races," was the next thing I said.

LW put a piece of sushi in his mouth as Val looked at me with a furrowed brow. "And what do you do?" Val asked Nathan.

"I manage musicians," he said.

"Barely," I said. "He only has one band." This part was true, but now it made me look like the asshole. And I had a feeling Val and LW weren't buying my story and I needed to do some damage control.

"I'm sorry, honey. I know you're trying, but what we do for a living isn't the problem. It's the time alone." I looked at Val and LW. "He never wants to have sex and when he does...well..." I drifted off so as to seem unsure about telling them.

"What is it, dear?" asked Val.

Nathan jumped in. "We have plenty of sex," he said haphazardly.

"Yeah, but not the way I like it," I said, then looked at Val and LW with a victim's pained expression. "All he ever wants to do is anal."

Nathan hopped up from the table and raced away as Val stared at me with horror in her eyes. LW lowered his head with one hand held over his forehead.

"I should go find my husband," I said and excused myself.

I strolled around for a few minutes, looking for David Stevenson. When I spotted him lingering by the buffet, I waved across the room and headed in his direction. He made a quick about-face and took off in the other direction.

I went looking for Nathan and found him standing in a corner, with his arms crossed, talking to an older gentleman. I took out my head scarf that I had since been using as a napkin, wrapped it around my forehead, and tied it in a big knot like an Indian chieftain. Then I sauntered up to Nathan and the man and said, "Hello, honey. Who is this you're talking to?"

"Oh, this was my dean, Dean Edwards." Nathan introduced us with a look that said, "Don't say *anything*," but I was over Nathan and I was over this party, so after a couple of minutes of small talk I leaned in.

"If you'll excuse me, gentlemen, I have to go take a dump."

Nathan and I met outside by the valet moments later, at which point we had no choice but to laugh uncontrollably until I actually started to wet myself. I hadn't peed in my pants in months! But that had been in Vegas and I was asleep so it didn't really count.

Exactly one week later, I went to a Lakers game on a date. As I walked down the aisle, I bumped directly into Larry William. "Hello, sweetie, how are you?" he asked.

"Oh, wow!" I said, "Hi! Your son must be playing against the Lakers." Larry nodded. "How are you?" I asked.

"Great. Are you here with your husband?" he asked, right in front of my date.

"No, actually we…" There was a long moment of uncomfortable silence, which LW, Val, and I had been through before, and then I said, "separated, we separated." Then I leaned in and whispered in LW's ear, "I think he's gay."

LW whispered back in my ear, "I think you might be right."

I introduced my date to LW and Val, and when we parted Val gave me a hug and whispered to me, "We'll pray for you."

"Please do," I responded.

My date and I went to find our seats. When we sat down he turned to me and said, "Well, that's *terrific* news. How long have you been married?"

Rerun

It was valentine's Day and I had spent the day in bed with my life partner, Ketel One. The two of us watched a romantic movie marathon on TBS Superstation that made me wonder how people who write romantic comedies can sleep at night.

At some point during almost every romantic comedy, the female lead suddenly trips and falls, stumbling helplessly over something ridiculous like a leaf, and then some Matthew McConaughey type either whips around the corner just in the nick of time to save her or is clumsily pulled down along with her. That event predictably leads to the magical moment of their first kiss. Please. I fall *all* the time. You know who comes and gets me? The bouncer.

Then, within the two-hour time frame of the movie, the couple meets, falls in love, falls out of love, breaks up, and then just before the end of the movie, they happen to bump into each other by "coincidence" somewhere absolutely absurd, like by the river. This never happens in real life. The last time I *bumped* into an ex-boyfriend was at three o'clock in the morning at Rite Aid. I was ringing up Gas-X and corn removers.

Usually, I like to celebrate Valentine's Day by hot-air ballooning around the greater Los Angeles area and pointing out all the different apartment buildings I've slept in. This Valentine's Day was different because I was still in a deep funk from being dumped by a man with skinnier legs than me. If you've ever seen the hind legs of a German shepherd trotting away from you, then you know what my ex-boyfriend's calves looked like.

I had been dating my landlord for about nine months before the breakup. He wasn't the Schneider of *One Day at a Time*–type of landlord, running around the building with a tool belt and a detective's mustache. He was a clean-cut, good-looking, bashful type of guy with a harmless disposition. He owned the building and the one directly next door, which he lived in. After meeting him for the very first time, while signing my lease, I called Ivory to give her the news. "I'm going to have to start dating my landlord."

"Really? Is he hot?" she asked.

"It's not *hot*. It's something else. He's shy and it's going to take some work. I think he might be scared of me. I'll have to wear him down."

And that's exactly what I did. I called him repeatedly with emergencies such as my pilot light going off (after I blew it out) and my sliding shower doors falling off their tracks (after I dislodged them). This would time and time again lead to coffee and/or a meal. After hanging out together for a couple of months and him not making a move, I finally confronted him. "Listen, landlord man, what's the story here? Are we going to start dating or what? I've got a crush on you and I'm not interested in any new friendships. The only reason I'm hanging out with you all the time is to get in your pants. And I'm exhausted." I had never put so much work into a relationship that hadn't even begun. "Either we become a couple or no more Chelsea."

"Let me think about it," he said.

Two days later he showed up at one of my stand-up shows. "You want to come back to my place?" he asked me afterward, as he walked me outside.

"Yes," I said and found myself skipping for the very first time since puberty.

My landlord was a soft-spoken type and we got along great—but we also fought a lot. He wasn't like any guy I had ever dated before. He was ultraconservative, insecure, and unsure of almost every decision he made. But at the same time he was also thoughtful, very funny, and really good at math. He wanted to spend almost every minute with me, which didn't annoy me like I thought it would.

We had completely opposite personalities. He would buy clothes, appliances, and supplies for the building and then, almost immediately, return them. This mentality drove me crazy. I didn't know men could be such flip-floppers. I had never returned anything in my life. If the item didn't work for me when I got home, then I would just throw my hands up and drop it off at Goodwill.

He always wanted the thermostat set at a minimum of seventy-five degrees; I would wake up in the middle of the night drenched in sweat and sneak out of bed to turn it below seventy. The next day, he would complain of a sore throat and tell me it felt like a meat locker. One morning I woke up to find him wearing a ski cap. So dramatic.

The worst things about him were his scrawny legs and the fact that I was pretty sure I could take him in a fight. He would cuddle so intensely with me in bed that when I'd get up to walk in the kitchen for a glass of water, he'd still be attached to me like an orangutan.

It wasn't the actual breakup that hurt so much. It was the fact that I had been planning on breaking up with him first but hadn't gone through with it because I thought he would be too devastated—only to come home from a weekend ski trip to Aspen and be blindsided. It was a complete blitz-krieg. I didn't appreciate the fact that I had been consider-ing someone else's feelings while he was telling *me* to hit the road. While I knew that the relationship could never work long-term, mostly because we would never be able to wear shorts together in public, I kept secretly hoping that maybe some new calf-enhancing technology was about to hit the marketplace.

A couple months went by but the pain didn't seem to be subsiding.

Ivory called on Valentine's Day to tell me there was a costume party that night and attendance was mandatory. "It's at a warehouse downtown and it's a fund-raiser to help children with disabilities." Finally, something I had been lying about doing for years could actually become a reality. I had no desire to leave my bed, but I had to pull through for the kids. "We're meeting at the Compound to preparty," Ivory said.

The Compound was the apartment building where Lydia lived with all of her degenerate neighbors. It was kind of a *Melrose Place*–type building minus the pool and six-figure incomes. It was a fun place to hang out and party, but not a fun place to wake up. Lydia and all of her neighbors had slept with each other at one time or another, and it had become an official lazy Susan.

"I don't have a costume," I told Ivory.

"We can make you one."

I reminded her of months earlier when, on Halloween, Ivory and I had gone as bull dykes, wearing black mullet wigs, huge Levi's jeans, chained wallets, and black-studded belts. Our wife-beaters read, "We Support Bush" and "Bush Rules." Since the party was after we had invaded Iraq, people thought we meant the president.

Not only did I learn my lesson that night about supporting George W. Bush in California, I learned my lesson about wearing something unattractive to a costume party. It was a clear opportunity to slut it out, and we had completely missed the boat. No one wanted anything to do with us. Even the friends we had gone to the party with were too embarrassed to be seen around us. Ivory and I spent the entire night sitting in a corner by ourselves; the only person who approached us was the bouncer to tell us it was last call.

"Oh, yeah, I forgot about that," Ivory said. "Go rent one."

"I can't. Bobby and Whitney's E! True Hollywood Story is on in ten minutes."

Ivory called minutes later to tell me her roommate Jen had an extra genie costume with a bustier that would look hot. "The pants are see-through, so wear full panties," she warned.

"I don't have any full panties, only my period underwear and those are too ugly."

"What color are they?"

"Red," I said. "Not from my period, they're just red."

They were nylon tummy tuckers and they sucked everything in when you were bloated. These weren't panties I wanted to show off. Generally, this type of underwear wasn't worn by anyone under sixty.

"No one will see them, it will be dark out, just wear something that covers your ass. Or wear a bathing suit bottom."

"What color are the pants?" I asked Ivory.

"Chelsea, just give it a rest. Be over at Lydia's by eight and we'll get ready there."

Parking at Lydia's was always a nightmare, so I called our friend Holden who lived around the corner and parked in his garage. Holden is like one of the girls. He's a sweet guy and we've all been friends with him for years. Holden's only fault is that he has a severe case of ADD. He's the type of person who asks you a question and then interrupts the answer with another question. This habit can be very annoying, especially if you're upset—which has resulted in many dramatic breakup scenes with his girlfriends involving clothes and furniture being thrown off balconies. Holden doesn't mind being yelled at, so that would help release the anger related to him not listening in the first place.

Holden didn't know about the party, probably because he wasn't paying attention when he got invited, so I invited him again. He didn't have a costume either, so I told him to wear one of his wet suits. Holden owns his own beach-wear company, where he sells everything from scuba suits to surfboards. He keeps all his equipment at his apartment, and it comes in handy every time I decide to spend more time underwater.

When I got to Lydia's place, all three girls were already dressed. Ivory was a sexy schoolgirl, Lydia was a sexy cop, and Jen was an M&M.

The genie costume was really cute and fit me perfectly. As soon as Jen saw it on me I caught a look on her face that said, "Take that off, I'm wearing it."

"Chelsea," Jen said. "I have an idea. You can be the M&M!"

"That's okay," I said. "You keep it. You like chocolate more."

"I insist," she said, grinning like one of those crazed cheerleaders after they've been hurled into the air. "And anyway, the genie's my costume in the first place. I brought it for you."

I put on the M&M suit. The top part was the shape of a pumpkin and formed a perfect green sphere around my body. It came with matching green tights that I wore over my red period panties. Jen's shoes for the M&M outfit didn't fit me and none of Lydia's shoes fit either. The only shoes I had with me were the ones I had worn over. Black Adidas slides. This became my outfit.

"I need your panties," Jen said while checking herself out in the full-length mirror. You could see right through her genie pants, and she was wearing a leopard thong.

"I'm not giving you my panties," I said, "and can we

please stop using that word?" There are three words that gross me out: "panties," "moist," and "slick." They all seem like words a child molester would use. Together.

"You need to give me them. I can't wear this outfit with a thong," Jen insisted.

"Fine!" I huffed as I took them off and put my tights back on.

"Don't you want some underwear?" Lydia asked.

"No, I'll just free-ball it." I wasn't in the business of borrowing other people's underwear and could not believe Jen was willing to wear mine.

"Do you want the green paint for your face?" Jen asked.

"No thanks," I said, shooting her a dirty look.

There's a fine line between being easygoing and being taken advantage of, and allowing someone to paint my face green would have been the latter.

"What's the matter? You look adorable," Jen said in the same voice you'd use talking to a girl who was going to her prom in a wheelchair.

Holden waddled up to me, wearing a scuba suit with a mask.

"I guess the two of us will be hanging out together tonight," I said.

The party had potential, but I never got into the swing of things due to my somber mood. Holden and I sat in a corner, making fun of people's costumes, and when we tired of that, I started making fun of Holden, who was sweating so profusely that he had taken down the top half of his scuba suit and was now topless.

At the end of the party, Lydia told us that we were all

going to after-hours at some guy in a Batman suit's apartment. The only selling point was that the apartment was
in Santa Monica, located conveniently around the corner
from Lydia's.

We were approaching the building when I thought it
looked eerily familiar. There are many apartment buildings
in Santa Monica that are nearly identical; I figured that
was the case here. But as Ivory, Jen, Lydia, Holden, and I
piled upstairs into Batman's apartment, I glanced around
the place and got a not so melancholy feeling. I never forget
an apartment. A face, maybe, but not an apartment. I eyed
Batman carefully but didn't recognize him at all.

"How long have you lived here?" I asked as I was checking my e-mail from his computer.

"About ten years," he told me.

"Do I look familiar to you?" I asked him as he handed
me a beer and I sat there in my M&M costume. I clicked
over to Oprah's website to see if they had decided on next
month's book.

"Not really. What's your name?"

"Chelsea."

"No. Maybe we've seen each other around."

After realizing that this after-party was going nowhere
fast, I went into the kitchen and made myself a bowl of Top
Ramen. Unfortunately, I had to eat it right out of the pot
with a pair of unused chopsticks, because I didn't spot a
dishwasher and judging by the looks of this place, he wasn't
a good cleaner. The girls were all sitting on his couch as
they listened to music. I was tired and reminded them that
nothing positive happens after two A.M.

Batman looked at me with devilment in his eyes and said, "That's not true."

I didn't like his tone and left the room. I walked into his bedroom and found a Nintendo box attached to his TV.

Nintendo had been replaced by PlayStation years earlier; I hadn't seen one of these boxes since middle school. The excitement I felt at that moment could be paralleled only by J. Lo releasing another album.

I was on level four of Super Mario Brothers when Ivory came in and told me that she thought Jen and Batman were going to hook up.

"She can't," I said. "I think I may have already slept with him."

"You did?"

"I'm not sure, but this place seems familiar."

Ivory left and got Lydia. They stood above me with their arms crossed, watching me play.

"Well, did you or didn't you?" Ivory asked.

"I don't remember, but I know I've been here, and I can't imagine sleeping over at a stranger's house without having sex with him." Then Batman walked into his bedroom holding a black piece of tar and asked if any of us were interested in smoking hash.

"Are you serious?" I said. The thought of smoking a brick had about as much appeal as seeing Michael Bolton perform live.

"Who smokes hash?" Lydia asked.

"Wait a minute. I know how I know you," I said.

Upon being offered hash, the memory flooded back. I was once partying late night at the Compound with some of Lydia's neighbors and Batman was there. He lived about ten blocks from me at the time, so we shared a cab home, but I was so drunk that when we stopped at his place, I got out as well. He didn't remind me that I didn't live there. When I walked inside and realized I was at his house, he leaned in and tried to kiss me. I told him to back off and get me a cold compress, a fan, and a pillow for his couch.

"I crashed here one night a couple of years ago, remember? I slept on your couch and you brought me a cold compress and a fan? Remember, I didn't feel so well?"

"Oh yeah, kind of...you were pretty wasted," he said.

"Oh, my God, that is so funny! Where was I?" Lydia asked.

"You were probably dating Ass Breath," I told her.

"Did you guys hook up?" asked Ivory.

"No, I just slept over," I said.

It was true: we hadn't had sex. I felt immense pride at that moment for having slept over at a stranger's house without hooking up. All of a sudden it was as if I were the mature one in our group of girls, and I made a note to myself to counsel them later on how "no means no!"

"Didn't you clean my apartment?" he asked me.

"Yeah, a little bit," I said. I had cleaned up because when I woke up in the morning, I couldn't believe the squalor this guy was living in. I am not a neat freak, so if I'm tidying up around someone's place, it's got to be pretty unsanitary. I distinctly remember there being cold cuts stuck to the wall.

"How did you remember sleeping here after a couple years?" Ivory asked me.

"Because he offered me hash that night too, and these are the only two times in my life that has happened."

"I can't believe you didn't sleep with him," Lydia said.

"Well, Lydia," I said very condescendingly, "sometimes you have to make smarter choices."

"Shut up, asshole," said Ivory.

"Can we go, or does Jen want to hook up with him?" I asked.

"Yeah, let's go. You wanna sleep at my place?" Lydia asked.

Holden, Ivory, Lydia, and I called a cab while Jen stayed behind. We got dropped off at the Compound and Ivory had the cab take her home. Holden walked to his apartment and I told him I'd come by in the morning for my car.

People were still up at the Compound partying. There was loud music playing and strangers were dancing in the courtyard.

"I'm going to bed," I told Lydia. "Give me your keys."

She looked through her purse for an amount of time that I knew could only result in her not having them. "Shit," she said. "I think I left them at Batman's or in the cab." She didn't seem bothered by this at all. "Oh, well. We'll figure it out," she said.

Lydia's neighbor Gary moseyed over in his cowboy costume to say hi. He tipped up his five-gallon hat and asked what was wrong.

"Lydia lost her house keys and I need to sleep," I said.

"My door's open," he told me. "Just go crash. I'll take the sofa."

"Great," I said. "Thanks, Dubya."

Not knowing Gary or his hygiene very well, I decided to keep my M&M outfit on. My tights and green rotunda would protect me from any potential bedbugs. I passed out and remember feeling Lydia climb into bed some time later that night and then someone else climbing into bed with us.

At around six in the morning I awoke to noises that can be associated only with heavy petting.

They were coming from the bathroom. Suddenly, there were loud crashes of what I presumed were toiletries falling to the floor.

"Oh! Oh! Oh, my God! G-G-G-G-Gary! Yes…right there, no, up more, oh, my GOD!" yelled Lydia.

Though I couldn't see myself, I knew I had the same look on my face that Macaulay Culkin had in *Home Alone* when he finds out that his parents have forgotten him.

I rolled out of bed, fell on the floor, and crawled out the door, keeping my head down like I was dodging enemy fire. I hadn't walked two steps outside before I realized I needed my cell phone, purse, and shoes. I tried the door. Locked. I knocked, but no one answered.

I looked around for any sign of life but quickly realized that at some point the night before I had taken my contacts out. Everything beyond twenty feet was blurry. This was not good. I paced back and forth, wondering what my next move would be, when I remembered my car was only blocks away at Holden's.

Could I walk the five blocks to Holden's in my M&M outfit? I knocked on the door of Gary's apartment again, but to no avail. I could still hear Lydia moaning. I felt as if I might become physically ill. This was a complete disaster. I couldn't believe Lydia would have sex while I was feet away in the same apartment. This wasn't high school!

Hearing your friend moaning someone's name during sex is down there with seeing your parents have sex. I know because, luckily for me, I had now experienced both.

There was no other choice. I ran down the steps of the complex and started sprinting along the sidewalk toward Holden's apartment. I stubbed my toe almost immediately, which slowed me to a brisk limp.

What I could barely make out as a woman walking her dog toward me crossed to the other side of the street upon seeing me. A guy in a passing car slowed down and yelled out the window, "Rough night?" This was humiliating. I had never been outside this early before and I didn't like the crowd.

It was one thing to wander around in an M&M costume on Halloween or maybe even the day after, but it was a whole other turn of events for me to be doing it in February. To make it worse, with every step, the thick cottony upper-body part of my costume, the actual M&M, kept riding up above my butt, and I kept having to hold it down with one hand behind my back. And this little M&M had to pee so badly.

When I arrived at Holden's, I immediately started throwing rocks at his sliding glass door. "Holden!" I screamed.

"Keep it down," one of his neighbors yelled, then came out on to his balcony. "Lady...oh." He paused. "How would you like it if I called the police?"

"Oh, please, go ahead," I said. "And tell them what, there's a crazy M&M outside?"

The neighbor shook his head and went back inside.

After what seemed like a year, Holden finally came

out, rubbing his eyes. As soon as he saw me, he burst out laughing.

"Can you just please come down and get me?" I said. More laughing. Now he was doubled over on his balcony, his face turning red.

"You know what, asshole? Can you laugh at me after I come inside instead of while I'm standing on a street corner?"

Holden went back inside only to come back out thirty seconds later with a camera. After his third snapshot of me at my worst, another neighbor appeared on a balcony. "Here we go again! Can't you and your girlfriends just give it a rest?"

That snapped Holden out of it. He went inside to open the door for me. "I'm not his girlfriend," I shouted up to his neighbor.

Holden came down and let me in. I went inside and peed for close to five minutes. This outfit was a disaster and the panty hose were starting to give me a rash.

"Take me home. I can break into my kitchen window," I told him.

I needed to be in my bed, at my house—now. I had been through enough humiliation for one day. And it was maybe time to start focusing on the path my life was taking.

We got to my apartment at around eight fifteen. I asked Holden to wait outside just in case I couldn't get in. It shouldn't be hard, I figured; since I lived on the first floor, all I had to do was push myself up to the kitchen window and climb through. I punched in the code to open the gate and made my way over to the kitchen window.

It was higher than I had remembered. I looked around nervously. I had never done this before. I knew it was possible because Lydia had done it once, but then again, she had help. Instead of going to get Holden, I tried on my own. It was unlocked, but I needed to hoist myself up in order to squeeze through. Halfway through, my M&M costume got stuck. The wiring that kept the shape of the M&M wouldn't budge. I either had to take it off my head or climb back down. If I took it off, I knew I could get in—I was already halfway there. So I squirmed out of the costume.

That's when I heard the back gate open and shut. There was the sound of approaching footsteps and then they stopped. Here I was with green tights and no underwear hanging out of my kitchen window with my head in my sink. "Holden, if you take a picture..."

"It's not Holden," said the voice of my ex-boyfriend/ landlord.

Shit. Shit. Shit. Please tell me this isn't happening to me.

"Do you need a hand, Chelsea?" he asked.

"No, thanks, I'm cool," I said offhandedly. As if people entered their apartments like this all the time.

He sighed deeply, ruffling his keys. Then he opened my door, entered the kitchen, and pulled me through. When I got to the floor I kneeled down with my arms around myself in order to cover my bra and my beaver, which you could easily see through my tights. He had taken the M&M part of the costume from outside and put it next to me.

My ex didn't say anything else, but he stared at me for what felt like an unnatural amount of time with a very calm, almost scary look on his face.

"It's not what you think..." I started to say. I wanted to tell him that despite appearances, I had actually been a very good girl last night and hadn't slept over at some guy's house and that really he should be applauding my heroic effort to get home. I wanted to explain everything, but judging by the look of despair on his face, I knew it would be pointless. It would all sound ridiculous.

"Just don't," he said. He went and got a towel, put it down next to me, and left.

I sat on my kitchen floor wondering what kind of people I was friends with. I also wondered if I was ever going to get married. After about an hour, I decided to stop feeling sorry for myself.

Why not look on the bright side? I had just spent my second night in bed with a stranger I hadn't had sex with. You don't have to be a genius to recognize that I was obviously on some sort of a roll.

FALSE ALARM

SHONIQUA AND I had somehow managed to get jobs working on the same television show. Now we were actually getting paid to act stupid, and we were very excited about it.

We were on a plane to San Francisco, where we would be shooting on location for three days. I was telling her about the latest humiliation with my ex and the M&M costume.

"Bitch, you're really gonna need to get your shit *together*," she said, as the flight attendant handed us warm peanuts. "Can you believe this ho?" she asked the flight attendant. "I bet *you're* not running around in Halloween costumes in the middle of winter losing *your* drawers."

The flight attendant smiled at Shoniqua, then looked over at me and frowned.

"Lower your voice," I told Shoniqua. "You don't have to tell me I'm an idiot, I already know that. The problem now is that the landlord thinks I've been sleeping around since we broke up and I haven't."

"Fuck him," she said. "He was a pussy, anyway. He didn't deserve your ass and I don't give a shit what he thinks."

"Thanks, Shoniqua."

"What I would like to know is when are you gonna realize that you're a grown-ass woman?" she asked me.

I had never heard anyone call me a "woman" before and it scared me. I still thought of myself as a little girl—or boy.

"What does that mean?" I asked her.

"I don't fucking know," she said. "Don't you want to get married?"

"Yes, of course I want to get married, but does that mean I'm not allowed to go out and have a good time? Am I supposed to just marry any schmuck that comes along? And by the way, here's a news flash, Hammer Toes. Nobody wants to marry me, anyway."

"You just love men too fucking much," she said. "You're like a man."

"You know what?" I told her. "It's better to get in the game and love men than to sit around on the sidelines complaining about them all the time like half of our girlfriends. Would you rather I was bitter and talked about how all men in L.A. are scumbags like everyone else in this town?" Now I was building momentum. "Have I ever once complained about being lonely or said that I was giving up? Have I?" I had started shouting and there were tears welling up in my eyes.

"All right, settle the fuck down with the crying. You obviously need to get some ass this weekend, and I'll get on it the minute this plane lands."

"Thank you," I said, relieved.

The flight attendant leaned into our row, looked at us disapprovingly, and asked us if we wouldn't mind keeping our voices down.

"I'm sorry," I told her. "She just got out of prison." Then Shoniqua made a gang sign and the flight attendant took off in the direction she came.

We landed in San Francisco and were driven to the W Hotel, where everyone working on the show was staying. We usually traveled with four or five producers, the director, and a couple of location scouts.

The three days went by pretty uneventfully due to fourteen-hour workdays.

On the last day we finished shooting early, at around five in the afternoon, so we met up with everybody at the hotel bar in the W. Everyone wanted to go out to dinner for our last night, but I was exhausted and told Shoniqua we should skip it.

Until this job, I had never experienced fourteen-hour workdays and my body was starting to shut down. Not only did I have a terrible work ethic mentally, it seemed my body was on the same page. I told everyone I was going to pass on dinner, when our producer Jeff informed me that one of his friends who lived in San Francisco was coming by to pick us up.

"He's good-looking, Chelsea," he said. "He's an attorney for the government, he's got a house and a boat, I think you'd like him. We'll all go to dinner."

I love how people list material items to get you interested in a person. I was just about to ask if Jeff's friend also had a bicycle but didn't have the energy.

"I'm too tired," I told Jeff. "I have no personality."

"Well, bitch, that's what I'm here for," Shoniqua jumped

in. "Chelsea, I think we should go. I'm tired too, but this could be worth it." That's the kind of friend Shoniqua is.

I shook my head, unconvinced.

"Listen, I *got* a husband, so it's up to you, but I would hate to see you miss an opportunity to get some booty. Especially from someone who sounds like marriage material."

The idea that our Neanderthal producer Jeff could actually have a friend who would be considered marriage material was about as likely as Paris Hilton winning a spelling bee. The conversations Jeff usually had involved two main topics: sex with animals and family pornography. Tonight, he had somehow steered the conversation to the new phenomenon of asshole bleaching when I excused myself to the ladies' room. I had eaten way too much during the last couple of days and had neglected to do any sort of exercise. I needed to see firsthand what kind of damage I had done to my midsection. I went into the bathroom, stood in front of a full-length mirror, and lifted up my shirt.

Good God. I looked like I was carrying a small baby. Not full term, just three or four months. Then I turned to the side for a second look. Clearly, I was well into my second trimester. I started going over baby names in my head. I liked the name Lucifer, but only for a girl. My stomach was in the beginning stages of overlapping my jeans—a few more days of this and I could apply for my plumber's license. I have a body like a Latin American; when I gain weight it distributes itself evenly, but only from the waist up. I turned back to face the mirror head-on. I looked like two sticks with a baked potato on top. "Ugh," I said aloud.

A woman exited one of the stalls and I asked her if she had ever seen anything like this.

"Are you getting your period?" she asked.

"I hope so," I said.

"Well, it's probably just water weight," she told me.

I knew it wasn't water weight because not only do I make it a personal rule never to drink water straight, I could actually see the outline of the cheeseburger I had eaten earlier that day. I made a mental note to get my hands on a Soloflex immediately upon my return to Los Angeles.

I went back to the bar and told Shoniqua that I was fat and therefore not in the mood to meet my prospective husband. "Another time," I said

That's when Carter walked in. I took one look at him and announced, "We're coming."

The first thing I liked about Carter was that he was wearing a suit. I love a man in a suit. Especially without the jacket. It reminds me of after-work cocktails at expensive restaurants. Living in Los Angeles for eight years and seeing men walk around in sweat suits and open-toed sandals in the middle of the afternoon will really make you respect a man with a job.

Carter was adorable, about six feet tall, and absolutely charming. He kissed us all hello and escorted the six of us out to his Yukon. I also like men with big cars. As we gathered in the backseat, Shoniqua pushed her index finger hard into my leg and said, "See, I fucking told you. It's a good thing you have me, cuz none of your white friends would go to bat for you like this."

We went to dinner at some Americanized Mexican restaurant and I tried to maneuver myself to sit directly across from him but somehow managed to sit in between two people I didn't even know were coming to dinner. But Shoniqua sat next to him, so I knew I was covered.

My dinner experience consisted of molesting a pair of enchiladas while listening to one of the local production assistants we hired tell me about finding her birth parents. I am always fascinated by adoption stories, but for different reasons than most. I am convinced my sister Sloane *was* adopted, and I have gone to great lengths to try and prove it. So far, I've been unsuccessful. The closest I came was when I hired an online attorney, who charged twenty-five dollars per e-mail and assured me there was a strong chance my blue-eyed, fair-skinned sister was of Creole descent.

After dinner we went back to the hotel bar for more drinks. Two of the people in our group excused themselves for the night, so our group had dwindled to five. Carter and I sat next to each other in overstuffed club chairs while the others were on the couch facing us. I was just finishing up my conversation with the production assistant when suddenly I heard the words "conspiracy theory."

There are two topics I enjoy even more than adoption: conspiracy theories and Jennifer Lopez. I turned my head so fast that my contact fell out.

Carter was discussing Kennedy's assassination. I bided my time and at the exact perfect moment interceded with, "Kennedy, Schmennedy, let's talk about Biggie Smalls and Tupac. That's where some real shit went down."

There were a couple of seconds of awkward silence before Shoniqua broke it for me. "Now you know you got that fucking right, Chelsea. Let's talk about it!"

Thanks to my segue, our group enjoyed a roundtable discussion, where everyone put their two cents in with regard to all three assassinations. This wasn't the first time I'd been able to bring people together and it was definitely something to think about. Maybe one day I would lead a committee for people who were unemployed but weren't looking to get back in the workforce.

Shoniqua said she was tired and going to bed. I gave her a look that said, "Don't go." She leaned down to kiss me good night and whispered, "It's on, he's into you. I fucking told his ass."

As soon as she left, Carter and I zoomed in on each other. While we were talking to the other guys with us, he kept putting his hand on my leg. I returned his affection with hard slaps to his back whenever anyone said anything funny.

I asked him about his job and he told me he prosecuted terrorists.

"Really?" I asked. "Do you work closely with President Bush?"

"I've met with him before, but mostly I work with his advisers."

"Does everyone just kind of sit around and make fun of him when he leaves the room, or is that kind of thing done on the quiet tip?"

He smiled and said, "No, I've never seen anyone make fun of him, but there are definite moments where looks are exchanged."

"Wait a second. Are you a Republican?"

"I'm registered as a Republican, but I don't always vote that way."

"Interesting," I said. "Very interesting."

I immediately had fantasies of marrying Carter and spending my free time with Colin Powell and Donald Rumsfeld at the Pentagon bar, where I would grill them about how they could be so opposed to stem-cell research yet not put a ban on the handlebar mustache.

I would convince them that gay couples deserved every benefit that the three of us were fortunate enough to have.

I would also talk to them about my 401(k) that I never started and see if they could somehow cut me a deal. There are so many issues I would lobby for in Washington, and I would make sure that everyone in my community was heard. I'd be like the new Jackie O, except wilder and I'd wear jeans.

I looked at Carter with a whole new level of respect and couldn't wait for us to start seeing each other more seriously. These feelings I had for him, coupled with the fact that I had just seen the episode of *Oprah* where she had a doctor on who explained that the more sex an individual had, the healthier they'd be, led me to my next decision. In my ever constant desire to maintain a healthy lifestyle, I decided it was time to make my move.

I got up and announced, "Well, everyone, I'm beat. I'm going up to my room. Carter, would you like to join me for a nightcap?"

"Of course," he said and stood up.

We stopped at the concierge's desk on our way to the elevator bank. "Would you mind sending up some ice to room 1202, please?" I asked.

"Sure thing, right away," he told me. Just as we were

about to step inside the elevator I ran back and whispered to the concierge, "Do you have any condoms?"

"Absolutely, Miss Handler," he said with a very professional smile. "I'll have them sent right up."

"Well, that was easy," I told Carter as I caught back up with him inside the elevator.

We weren't alone in the elevator so we didn't start kissing until we got into my hotel room. It wasn't immediate, though, because first Carter headed straight to the minibar and took out every bottle of alcohol.

There was a couch that ran the length of the window and was connected to the wall. We sat on it together while he poured me a warm vodka and soda and a gin and tonic for himself. Then he went to the fridge and took out a sixteen-dollar bottle of VOSS water and chugged it.

"Are you okay?" I asked him.

"Yeah, I'm just so parched."

"Yeah, I guess."

"Oh, I'm sorry. Do you have to pay for any of this?" he asked.

"No, don't worry about it. Have some Pringles too if you want."

"That's okay." He smiled.

We made out for a little bit, which was pretty blasé. We didn't have the chemistry I was hoping we would, and I was sensing Carter wasn't able to relax. He kept getting up and sitting back down. He was a really nice guy and charming, but his body language was all over the place. Then we heard a knock at my door. He tipped the bellhop and grabbed the ice bucket along with a sunglasses case.

"What is this?" he asked as he opened it and saw three condoms splayed inside like magazines at a doctor's office.

"Did you order condoms?" he asked me.

"No, are those really condoms?" I asked. "That is so funny. Talk about good hotel service."

Carter was emptying ice into our glasses while I turned on the satellite radio. I went to the bathroom to freshen up and take a last look at my gut. I wasn't happy with it, but I had noticed that Carter's body wasn't in tip-top condition either and he was carrying a little extra meat around the middle. He had the physique of a football player who had stopped playing years earlier.

I brushed my teeth and came out. Carter was sitting on the window sofa when I approached. He made a movement with his mouth that I immediately recognized from my friend Nathan's drug-induced repertoire. It indicated one of two things: either he had a hair in his mouth or he was on cocaine. It was not at all attractive and I needed to investigate further.

"Are you partying right now?" I asked.

He hesitated and then said, "I just did a tiny little line. Is that okay?"

"I don't know. Is this going to affect your performance?" I asked, referring to his penis.

"No, no, not at all," he replied.

Carter took this as his cue to prove to me that he was indeed ready for some action and threw me on the bed. He got on top of me and started to put his hand up my shirt when I moved it down the back of my pants instead. I wanted my torso quarantined until I could get into the perfect horizontal position with my hands over my head to ensure a leaner look.

"Your butt is so cute," he said as he squeezed it a little too hard.

"You think that's good, wait until you get a load of these!" I said as I threw off my shirt and undid my bra.

"Wow," he said.

"Don't look, feel!" I told him, as I forced his head between the girls.

Then he moved his head down my stomach. I stretched out farther and farther and he set off for downtown.

I quickly pulled him back up. I don't like oral sex between strangers and had to redirect focus. I undid his pants, and he tried again with his head to travel in a southerly direction.

"No," I said. "Let's have sex."

I yanked Carter's pants off and he reached for one of the condoms that he had placed on the nightstand. We were rolling around a little until he put one on and headed in the direction of my vagina.

A moment went by while I waited for him to get started. Instead, he just laid on top of me in silence. Was this Carter's idea of sex?

"What's up?" I asked.

"I'm really sorry," he said. "I don't think I can get it going."

"What?" I asked.

"I did a little more than one line...but I can do other things," he said.

I wondered if by other things he meant finding me someone with a working penis.

"I feel like shit," he said.

"Ugh," I said and put my hand over my forehead. "Don't you work for the government?" I asked.

"Yes," he said.

"Well, what do you guys do, just sit around and blow lines together? Is that what's taking place in our nation's capital?"

"No, no, not at all."

"This is ridiculous," I said and rolled over to cover myself with the comforter.

"Can I come to L.A. and make it up to you? This doesn't usually happen," Carter explained.

Come to L.A? I thought.

I was so irritated by the whole situation. I hadn't even wanted to go out in the first place tonight, and now look what happened. I consumed way more than my allotted fifteen-hundred-caloric intake, all in the name of sex, and now I wasn't getting any.

"I'm going to sleep," I told him.

"I'm leaving my number for you. I'd like to see you again if you're not too turned off."

"Great," I said with the same enthusiasm I reserve for Steven Seagal movies.

I woke up the next morning and found Carter's cell number scribbled on a hotel pad. I packed my things in order for our airport pickup at nine a.m. At eight, I went down to the restaurant and ordered an egg white omelet with a side of Tabasco. I needed to get serious about the couple of extra pounds I had packed on. I sat at a table by myself, reading Dear Abby. When in doubt, advice about lending out a hairbrush will always put things in perspective.

The thought occurred to me that the one-night stand was not nearly as much fun as it used to be. I felt disgusted with myself for being so disappointed in a complete stranger not being able to perform. I felt like a man must feel after using and abusing women for ages. Then I reminded myself that I had only physically hit one man, and he had seemed to enjoy it. I felt better, but was still low. What am I doing, I thought.

If I continued on this path, the only men I was going to meet were guys like me, and I definitely don't want to end up with someone like me. The idea of marriage and monogamy were concepts that didn't make me shiver like they once used to. I wanted someone like Shoniqua had, to call when I was traveling or to come back to after happy hour ended.

The thought of giving up alcohol crossed my mind too, but I was soon reminded of the promise to Ketel One, Grey Goose, and other top-shelf vodkas I had made in my early twenties. Never turn your back on someone who has asked nothing in return.

These were feelings I had felt coming on in the past couple of years that I repeatedly pushed to my subconscious for fear of my very first panic attack.

I felt like maybe it was time to grow up, and I was *not* happy about it.

Shoniqua, of course, came down at ten minutes past nine because she had never been on time in her life. I was already in our idling car when the driver opened the door for her. She hopped in. "What's up, ho?! How was it?"

"Don't ask."

"What? Girl, please don't tell me you managed to fuck it up. I put in a good two to three hours workin' that shit out for you. Do *not* tell me you somehow managed to fuck that up."

"Carter does coke and couldn't get it up."

Her mouth stayed open until I physically closed it for her.

"I think you should give him another chance," she said. "Did you give him your number?"

"He gave me his and it's still upstairs where I left it."

"Chelsea," Shoniqua said in her shame-on-you voice.

"I've decided I'm taking a break," I told her.

"A break from what?" she asked.

"Sex. I'm not having sex for a while, or at least until I meet someone I care about. I'm done."

"Well, shit, I've never heard you say that before," Shoniqua said. "You might go into fucking shock."

"It's not fun anymore, and you're right. I'm an actual grown-up and whether I like it or not, someone is going to have to marry my ass one day so I better start getting ready for him."

"Copy *that*!" Shoniqua said.

"Did you hear that, Ahmed?" she said to the driver, whose name she didn't know. "Chelsea's closing up shop for the winter! Well, it's about fucking time!"

We were flying to New York City to film some more of our television show, so my father decided to pick us up from the airport and bring us home for dinner.

"I can't wait to see your hot mess of a daddy," Shoniqua said as we collected our luggage from the baggage claim.

We walked outside and I spotted my father standing

halfway out of a purple two-doored Ford Escort with racing stripes. The front fender was missing, and having grown up with vehicles like this parked in our driveway for years at a time, I was able to deduce that the car was from somewhere between 1980 and 1985. We were in the year 2005.

"There's Melvin." I pointed.

"Where, where?" She looked around excitedly.

"Right there."

"Look at *that* piece-of-shit car," she said.

Melvin saw us heading in his direction, leapt out the driver's side door, and started waving.

"Do you see those fucking sausage fingers attached to his hands?" Shoniqua asked, smiling and waving back.

He came around the door so we could see his complete outfit. He had on dark sunglasses that took up half of his face and a tan cowboy hat that barely fit his head. He was wearing a huge multicolored sweater covered in grease stains that my mother had undoubtedly knit for him over a red golf shirt whose collar was exposed. Completing his look were cargo pants held up by suspenders and Velcro high-top sneakers.

"Look at him, look at him..." Shoniqua repeated several times over. "What up, Melvin?!" she screamed and ran in his direction.

"How's my black magic?" he asked her as he went in for a kiss on the lips and she turned her face in order for it to land on her cheek.

"Look at you!" she said. "This is a *hot* car."

"You like it?" he asked.

"Like it? It matches your sweater," she said as she

hopped into the front seat. I went around my father's side, endured his kiss on the lips, climbed in the back, and wiped my mouth.

"You wouldn't believe it, but this car has a hundred and fifty thousand miles on it," my father told us.

"It looks brand new," I said.

"What's up with the fender, Melvin? What happened to that?"

"Oh, who cares? That's aesthetics. You don't need a fender for a car to work. I've had this car in the paper for three days and have already had ten calls. It's gonna go quick."

Shoniqua turned her head to make eye contact but I focused on the traffic.

"So how was the trip?" he asked. "Did you keep Chelsea out of trouble?"

"Yeah, you know me, I try and keep her ass on the straight and narrow," she told him.

"She's gotta be very careful, my daughter. Men love her. And she *loves* men. She's *very* attractive, just like her daddy."

I pressed my face up against the window in order to focus hard on something else.

"Yeah, she sure is, just like her *daddy*," Shoniqua said. She poked her finger behind his seat and into my leg. She does this all the time, and on occasion I've bruised from it.

"You know, when I was younger—not so much anymore— women were very drawn to me," he said. "I've lived in several parts of the world—Italy, Spain, Greece, Germany— and I was quite a ladies' man back in the day."

"Back in the day?" Shoniqua asked.

"Yeah, back in the day...quiet tip, I know what all the young people are saying these days, I get MTV, I watch *The Real World*."

"*Really?*" she asked.

"Oh yeah," he said, just as his cell phone went off playing Usher's "Confessions" as its ring.

"Okay," Shoniqua said and threw her purse at my head. "This motherfucker is crazy," she hissed through clenched teeth.

Melvin was on the phone with a prospective buyer. "...Mint condition, purrs like a baby, AM/FM stereo, manual windows, spoiler, all the bells and whistles... twelve seventy-five is what I'm asking. No negotiating!"

"He wasn't serious about buying a car, people don't know what they want," he said as he hung up on the person. "So anyway, Chelsea's mother ordered some Chinese for you girls." He turned to Shoniqua as he drove over a curb. "Unless you want us to pick up some chicken on the way back."

"I'm good with Chinese," she said as she tightened her grip on my kneecap. I didn't know how much more of this I could take and Shoniqua now had her window open with her head sticking out of it.

"You girls want some AC?" my father asked. "The AC's powerful, just put in some new coolant." He went on. "Anyway, like you were saying, I had my heyday too once, women were just drawn to me...still are in a way. Sometimes I'll go to the market and three or four different women will ask me where to find anything from pickles to peaches. I feel sorry for the ladies, probably widows...they see a man like me, don't know what to do with themselves. Chelsea's the same way, can't keep her away from the men or the men away from her."

Shoniqua blew her nose and somehow managed to comport herself. "I think Chelsea's going to be taking a break from men for a while," she said. "I'm gonna try and get her ass a husband."

"Really?" my father asked.

"That's right. She's twenty-eight now, she needs to start focusing on being an adult."

"Well, I'm glad she's got someone like you looking out for her. God knows she's never listened to me or her mother."

"You got that right, Melvin. I'll straighten her ass out. She could write a book about all the men she's been involved with."

"That's not a bad idea, Shoniqua. That could be catchy."

"You hear that, Chelsea." She turned and looked at me. "You should write a book."

"What a dumb idea," I said.

ACKNOWLEDGMENTS

Michael Broussard, Colin Dickerman, Stephen Morrison, Marisa Pagano, Mark Schulman, Susan Haber, Matt Johnson. Chet, Roy, Glen, Simone, Shana, Olga, Wideload, Mikey, Black Magic, and all my nuggets. Aunt Gaby and Uncle Terry Burke for all my vodka. Panio Gianopoulos, thank you very much for all of your work, very nicely done. Except for the day you went to the "chiropractor."

ABOUT THE AUTHOR

Chelsea Handler is the star of the E! hit series *Chelsea Lately* and its spinoff comedy series, *After Lately*, as well as the #1 bestselling author of *Chelsea Chelsea Bang Bang*; *Are You There, Vodka? It's Me, Chelsea*; and *My Horizontal Life*. You can visit her online at Facebook.com/ChelseaHandler and follow her on Twitter @chelseahandler.

More from A Chelsea Handler Book/ Borderline Amazing® Publishing

Available now

What's so funny?

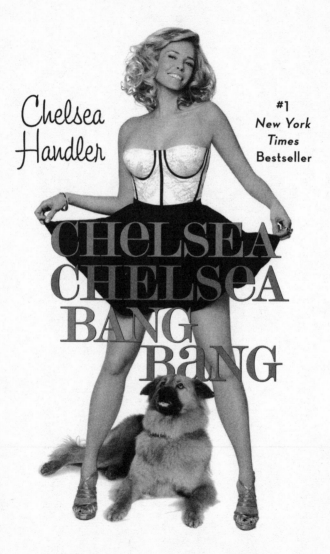

Chelsea
Handler

#1
New York
Times
Bestseller

CHELSEA
CHELSEA
BANG
BANG

Pick up a copy today.